*The* **Prayer**
*He*
**Taught**

# The Prayer He Taught

Seven dramas & meditations on the Lord's Prayer

## W. A. POOVEY

AUGSBURG PUBLISHING HOUSE
MINNEAPOLIS, MINNESOTA

*To Virginia.*
*Marrying you*
*was the best idea*
*I ever had.*

THE PRAYER HE TAUGHT

# Contents

# *Preface*

Jesus gave the Lord's Prayer to the disciples more than 1900 years ago. Since that time it has been repeated more times than human calculators can count. Christians in every land, using almost every known language, have framed their wishes through the words of this prayer. Whether Jesus intended his words to be used over and over again in Christian worship as we do, no one can tell. But the prayer is a basic part of Christianity.

Unfortunately, too often we repeat the Lord's Prayer without taking time to consider what we are saying. It is almost inevitable that anything used so often will sometimes be repeated without thought to its meaning. But there is no reason we should not recapture some of the deep truth contained in these ancient words.

The plays and the meditations in this book represent an effort to bring alive the petitions of the prayer. Each play is an entity in itself and can be presented without any relationship to a series. This is particularly true of the last play. Although it is intended for production during the Easter season, its message would be appropriate for any part of the church year.

Each petition is treated separately except for two, "And lead us not into temptation, but deliver us from evil." These seem to belong together, so one play is used to express both truths. The last play is based on the doxology.

Many characters in the dramas can be played by either women or men. Keep in mind that the plays can be altered to match your circumstances.

The meditations are brief, simple suggestions for the pastor who wishes to use a sermon with the play. It is possible to present the plays without comment or to follow them with a discussion period.

If this book helps to make us think a little deeper as we pray the words of the Lord's Prayer, it will have served the author's purpose.

*Our Father
who art in heaven,
Hallowed be thy name.*

**Matthew 6:9**

| | |
|---|---|
| DRAMA | *Hallowed Be Thy Name* |
| MEDITATION | *The Invisible God* |

# Hallowed Be Thy Name

CHARACTERS

THE REV. MATT BENDER: fairly young, rather lively minister

CORA BENDER: Matt's wife; concerned, serious, but with
a sense of humor

STUDENT: Teenager, serious; male or female

FARMER: rather loud, about Matt's age

(Note: The effectiveness of the play can be increased by
having the local minister and his wife play the parts of
Matt and Cora Bender.)


SETTING

The scene is the study of the Rev. Matt Bender. There is
an easy chair and a table piled with books. Other furniture
can be added as desired.

(As the play begins, MATT is pacing back and forth, apparently in deep study. After a few minutes, the door opens
and CORA appears.)

CORA: Matt, for goodness sake, what's going on! You're shaking the whole house with your pacing. I'm afraid you're going to wear out the floor and come tumbling down on my head!

MATT: I'm sorry, Cora. I didn't realize I was disturbing you. I'll try to be quieter in the future.

CORA: Oh, I really didn't mind. But I can't get my work done because I keep wondering what's going on up here. Are you trying to decide whether to buy me a new fur coat, or are you planning to marry a new wife?

MATT: Silly. If you must know, I'm having a rough time with my sermon for Sunday.

CORA: Having trouble trying to decide who to bawl out this week? Maybe you could take a swing at nosy preachers' wives!

MATT: *Cora!*

CORA: Sorry, dear. Just teasing you a little. But I don't understand why you're having trouble. I thought you announced that you were going to preach a series of sermons on the Lord's Prayer, starting this Sunday.

MATT: I did, worse luck. Remind me never to announce a new series until I've figured out what I'm going to say. At least I should have the first sermon down cold before I take the plunge.

CORA: But Matt, the Lord's Prayer! That should be easy for you.

MATT: *(Bitterly.)* Should be. Unfortunately it isn't. This week I'm supposed to be explaining the opening section—"Our Father who art in heaven, hallowed be thy name." *(Holds up a blank piece of paper.)* See—that's as far as I've gotten.

CORA: Matt, that's ridiculous! I'm not a seminary graduate, but even I know the Bible has hundreds of passages about God. Can't you just choose one and explain it? How about—"The heavens are telling the glory of God; and the firmament proclaims his handiwork"? That ought to be a good starting point. And if you don't like that passage, there are plenty of others.

MATT: You're very helpful, Cora. But I've studied dozens of texts. I looked up the word "God" in my concordance and almost read myself blind. The person who invented small print must have had a hard time getting into heaven—*if* he got there. But every passage seems hollow when I sit down to study it.

CORA: Hollow? That's a funny word to use about the Bible.

MATT: I can't think of a better one. This business about God ruling in heaven and human beings hallowing and praising his name seems meaningless to me right now. I suppose it was easy to put those two ideas together when heaven was just above the clouds and God's only business was supposed to be taking care of this earth. But we've got a different picture now.

CORA: I don't understand what you're trying to say.

MATT: It's very simple. God's a thousand times bigger than human beings ever dreamed he was. He has millions, even billions of stars to be concerned about. There are whole galaxies millions of light-years away that dwarf our own universe. I'm afraid we'll have to admit that this earth is just a speck in God's eye, just a floating bit of dust in space. How can I make people feel close to God today? How can I tell them to hallow his name? God is too big, too far from us now. What can I say about such a God in a 15-minute sermon? Tell me, Cora.

CORA: I'm sorry, dear. I'm no theologian. If you don't know the answer, I can't be much help. But I suspect you're too tired to think right now. After all, you were out late last night. That meeting went on until after 11. Why don't you settle down in your chair and take a little cat-nap? I'm sure it would do you a world of good.

MATT: Cora, I have to get this sermon written. Sunday comes after Saturday every week, whether we preachers like it or not. *(Thinks.)* Still, maybe you're right about that nap. I am a little tired. Suppose I try to catch 40 winks.

CORA: Good.

MATT: But you have to promise to come back and wake me up in 10 minutes. I've got to get this sermon finished.

CORA: All right. I promise. But you settle down right now. And no cheating by getting back to work the minute I leave the room!

MATT: No cheating, dear. *(He settles down as* CORA *exits. He is asleep almost at once. In a few seconds* CORA *comes back and covers him up with a blanket, then tiptoes away.)*

STUDENT: *(Appears rather suddenly. If possible, throw a light on him to indicate this is a dream sequence.)* Matt, Matt Bender.

MATT: *(Sits up but obviously is still asleep.)* What, What? Somebody calling me? *(Becomes aware of* STUDENT.*)* Who are you?

STUDENT: Just a figure in your dream, a bit of the past floating in the back of your mind. But I'm here to help you with that sermon of yours, if you'll take my help.

MATT: I'll take any help I can get. It's an awful feeling to face Saturday night and have nothing ready for Sunday. But what can you tell me about hallowing God's name?

STUDENT: Nothing too deep or theological. I'm only a high school student, and not the brightest one in my class, either.

MATT: Just like me at your age.

STUDENT: *(Meaningfully.)* That's right, just like you. This term I'm taking a course in astronomy at school. It was supposed to be a snap, but it hasn't turned out that way.

MATT: I remember that course. I took it years ago. And it wasn't a snap then either. But what's that got to do with my sermon? *(To audience.)* Oh, the crazy things a person dreams.

STUDENT: Tell me, how much do you remember about that course in astronomy?

MATT: Not much, I'm afraid. My knowledge has all evaporated.

STUDENT: Still, a few minutes ago you were talking about millions of light-years and billions of stars just as if you knew all about it.

MATT: I guess that was just a little bit of preacher talk. But was I so wrong?

STUDENT: Not really. This *is* a tremendous universe that we live in. The teacher has certainly made us see that. But you've forgotten something that you should have learned in that class.

MATT: What's that?

STUDENT: Simply that the one who made those billions of stars made you too. He not only put the stars in the sky, but he gave you eyes to see them and a mind to grasp the mysteries of the universe.

MATT: You're right. I *had* forgotten that.

STUDENT: You shouldn't have. Look—I found the notebook you used when you took astronomy course number 201. And it contains some interesting comments.

MATT: Good heavens! I forgot all about that old notebook. It must contain a lot of nonsense.

STUDENT: It does. There are doodles on almost every page, and now and then a girl's name and phone number.

MATT: Don't let Cora see that notebook!

STUDENT: Don't worry. The notebook isn't any more real than I am. But listen to what you wrote then. *(Reads.)* The God who made the stars also notes the fall of a sparrow and clothes the lilies of the fields. He made the blazing sun and also the microscopic creatures in a drop of water. Praise be to God! Hallowed be his name!

MATT: I did write that, one day right after the teacher had given an especially good lecture. It's beginning to come back to me now. I guess I didn't sleep all the time in class.

STUDENT: Maybe your own words have something to say to you about why we should hallow God. Maybe he isn't as far away from us as you seem to imagine.

MATT: You're making wonderful sense. I'm beginning to see. . . . (STUDENT *disappears.)* Why— why, where are you? Don't leave me now. Just when I'm beginning to understand. *(Reaches for him, falls back.)* Oh my dreams, my dreams.

FARMER: *(Appears suddenly.)* Hey there, preacher. I want to talk to you.

MATT: Who—who are you?

FARMER: I'm a farmer—the farmer you might have been if you hadn't decided to study for the ministry.

MATT: That's right! I did think I might take up farming, once, long ago. *(Looks at hands.)* I'm afraid these soft hands wouldn't last long on a farm now.

FARMER: Soft hands can be toughened up in a hurry. It's your soft head that'd get in the way.

MATT: *(Surprised.)* What did you say?

FARMER: I'm a figure in your dream so I don't have to be polite. I say you've got a soft head.

MATT: You're probably right. But what brought you to that startling conclusion?

FARMER: I heard that stuff you were saying about God being far off somewhere. And that's nonsense.

MATT: Is it? *(Sarcastic.)* You've received some special revelation from on high, have you?

FARMER: You might put it that way. Any farmer with his eyes open could tell you preachers some things about God. We see him at work every day, while you just *talk* about him on Sunday.

MATT: I see. You're going to give me a lecture now, I suppose?

FARMER: Not exactly. But it's stupid to talk about the world and miss the most important part of it—God himself. Only maybe you don't want to hear anything from me. I'm not a theologian or a philosopher either.

MATT: If you can help me with my sermon for Sunday, I'll listen, even if you're a dunce.

FARMER: All right. Look here. (MATT *looks as* FARM-
ER *opens hand and shows him some seeds. Wheat
or rice can be used.)* See those? They're seeds.
Bits of matter, parts of the elements of this
world. They don't look like much. *(Takes one.)*
They don't taste like much either, until you
cook them. But somebody put something alive
into those seeds and gave them the power to
grow. And when I plant them in my field and
the rain falls on them and the sun warms them,
I get a bumper crop. That's the way the world's
fed. I have to take care of things to get a good
crop, of course, but God does most of the work.

MATT: Oh, come now. You're just talking about the
forces of nature. I know all about that, even if
I am a soft-headed preacher.

FARMER: Calling God the forces of nature doesn't
change anything. I tell you, God's on my farm,
working with me and making everything grow.
God touches the apple trees and makes them
bear blossoms and fruit. He touches the cows
and they produce milk and cream out of green
grass and water. God's there all the time, working even when I'm asleep. I ought to say hello
to him every morning and thank him every
night for what he does for me.

MATT: Are you saying God is your hired hand? Because if you are—

FARMER: Not for a minute. *I'm* the hired hand. He's
the one running the world. You wise guys have
been trying to bow him out of his universe, but

he won't leave. He's still here, caring for us and feeding and clothing us. Look around you, man. Quit sitting in your study reading your books, and start seeing him in the world he's made for us. He may be on that far-off star, and he may be guiding a comet through his sky. I don't know about those things. But he's as near to me as the seeds in my hand and the soil on my farm.

MATT: Maybe you're right. Maybe I've just been thinking and speculating too much and not looking at the real things of the world. (FARMER *disappears.*) Tell me some more. Why — why — where did you go? Where are you? *(Sinks back.)* I'm only talking to myself in a dream. I — I —

CORA: *(Appears in dream.)* Matt, Matt —

MATT: Cora! Is it time for me to wake up already? Did you come to tell me to get back to work on that sermon?

CORA: No, Matt. I'm another figure in your dream right now. I'm here to remind you of something that happened more than 20 years ago. Do you remember the date June 15th?

MATT: Of course I do. That's Jack's birthday.

CORA: Right the first time. Now try to remember all that happened on that day 20 years ago.

MATT: That's not hard to do. I'll never forget our frantic rush to the hospital, and how hard it was for you that night, and how I paced the hospital floor—even more than I've been pacing my study tonight.

CORA: Was that all you did? Just walk back and forth?

MATT: You know it wasn't. I prayed. Oh God, how I prayed! Everything I had ever hoped for was wrapped up in you and that child struggling to be born. I don't suppose I ever prayed so hard before or since.

CORA: Why did you pray, Matt?

MATT: Because I wanted God's help for you. For all of us. Because I didn't have any place else to turn.

CORA: Strange that you should pray to a God so remote, so far away that he isn't concerned about this world.

MATT: I — I —

CORA: But it seems like your prayers were answered. Jack was born and I came through that night all right. But remember how tiny Jack was? Just an armful of struggling flesh.

MATT: He certainly was. He was one of the smallest, most helpless babies I've ever seen.

CORA: But *we* took care of that, didn't we? *We* fed him and taught him to walk and talk. *We* pulled him through sicknesses and accidents. *We* took care of his education and even saw to it that he learned to believe in God and that he grew up to be a faithful Christian. Didn't *we*, dear?

MATT: I seem to detect some sarcasm in that little word "we."

CORA: Why should you think that?

MATT: Because *we* didn't do it. Not by ourselves. You know as well as I do that it wasn't our doing that brought Jack through his first 20 years of life. *We* didn't pull him out of that terrible sick spell he had when he was five years old. *We* gave up hope. Even the doctor thought he wouldn't make it. But God healed him. God was with him then.

CORA: Maybe you're right. And do you think God had any part in making him grow or helping him learn? Do you think God was involved when Jack accepted Jesus Christ as his Savior?

MATT: Of course, of course. I guess God did it all. We weren't always the best parents in the world, Cora. I was too strict and you were sometimes too easy on the boy. But God was with him and that made up for all of our mistakes.

CORA: Strange, isn't it, what that far-away God gets done?

MATT: Oh, Cora, I've been blind, stupid, foolish. (CORA *exits.*) I've been looking for God in the depths of space when he was so near to me. I've talked about galaxies when I should have been thinking about people under my own roof. (*Realizes she is gone.*) Why — why — where are you? (*Struggles to get awake.*) Cora, Cora, I've been dreaming. (*Shouting.*) Cora, Cora.

CORA: (*Reappears.*) Matt, you don't have to shout

so loud. I was just coming to wake you up. But I guess I don't need to. Have you really been asleep?

MATT: Asleep? Yes, in more ways than one. But weren't you here a few minutes ago, standing there talking about Jack?

CORA: Matt, I just this minute came through the door. You must have been dreaming. *(Reflective.)* Dreaming about me. How nice.

MATT: It was nice, but not quite the way you mean it. Cora, I've got my sermon for tomorrow. I dreamed it all in the past 10 minutes.

CORA: Well, don't tell the church board you're writing your sermons by dreaming them. You'll never get a raise in salary that way.

MATT: Right now I don't care about a raise or anything else except that I know what I'm going to say tomorrow. And if I can only say it right, everyone in the church will know what we mean when we say—"Our Father who art in heaven, hallowed be thy name."

# The Invisible God

"Our Father who art in heaven,
Hallowed be thy name."

In his explanation of the First Commandment,
Martin Luther said, "We are to fear, love, and trust
God above anything else." That seems like a tall
order, particularly when you consider that we cannot see God, we cannot feel him, we cannot meet
him face to face. As the Lord's Prayer reminds us,
God is in heaven, and that signifies separation from
us, distance, remoteness.

Human beings have always felt this separation.
Moses wanted to see God face to face. The disciples
asked Jesus to show them the Father. Pagan people always carved idols or painted pictures to represent God because they felt the need for something
tangible, something divine they could see and touch.

Jesus' declaration that God is a spirit does not
bring God any closer to us. Indeed, this remoteness, this sense that God is not visibly present with
us makes many people deny his very existence. It is

the fool, of course, who says there is no God, but there is a certain logic about this foolishness.

Yet in the Lord's Prayer we say, "Hallowed be thy name." How can we be expected to hallow and respect someone who is so remote from us? Perhaps the answer lies in a simple inscription found on the tomb of Sir Christopher Wren. Wren designed and built St. Paul's Cathedral in London and later was buried in that church. His tomb is a simple one, but it contains the inscription: "If you seek a monument, look about you." The whole Christian church is a monument to its divine architect.

That's a good answer to our problem about God. We may not be able to see him, but the evidences of his power and nature are all around us. Examine the world which God has made. Observe the intricate and beautiful designs in the universe. Everywhere you look, from the giant galaxies to the structure of a single atom, there is clear indication that a master designer planned this world. The communist Whittaker Chambers confessed that he first began to doubt his atheistic doctrines when he noted the delicate convolutions of his daughter's ear. Of course it is easy to deny this evidence from design, but for those who are truly seeking God, the world bears witness of his presence. This is our Father's world.

But there are other evidences of God's existence too. The history of Israel as recorded in the Old Testament speaks eloquently of God. The story there tells how God took a small, insignificant group of people and made them the greatest religious force in human history. Time and again Israel failed God, but

God never failed in his promises. He finally let his people go into exile, but he promised to rescue them and he did. He told them that he would send a savior, and in due time God's Messiah appeared. The record of God's actions is plainly recorded in the Old Testament for all to see. Of course, it can all be explained away as coincidence and boastfulness on the part of Israel, but for those willing to read the evidence, the Bible shows clearly the hand of God in human history.

As Christians we see God most clearly revealed in Jesus Christ, who gave us the Lord's Prayer. Jesus Christ is God's illustrated sermon to the world. Jesus is God saying, "This is the way I am." When the disciples asked to see the Father, our Lord told him that if they had seen him, they had seen God. The writer of Hebrews says of Jesus: "He reflects the glory of God and bears the very stamp of his nature" (1:3). When we see Jesus healing the sick, welcoming little children, condemning the super-pious, and even suffering and dying for human beings, we see God. The Father's signature is written clearly on all that Jesus did.

And yet, and yet. . . . God still remains the Father who is in heaven. We can see the evidences of God, yet he remains the great mystery for us. He is, as the hymn writer put it: "Immortal, invisible, God only wise, In light inaccessible hid from our eyes." Indeed, we are often like Job, who cried out in his search for God: "Behold, I go forward, but he is not there; and backward, but I cannot perceive him; on the left hand I seek him, but I cannot behold him;

I turn to the right hand, but I cannot see him"
(23:8, 9).

When we really get down to cases, our faith in
God is just that: faith. We believe in God. We trust
that he exists and that he cares for us. Thus when
we pray the Lord's Prayer, we are speaking in faith.
We are indicating with our first words that we believe in the God whom we cannot see or know in a
tangible, physical way.

And this faith in itself is the hallowing of God's
name. Basically we hallow God when we put our
trust in him, when we believe in him enough to
worship him. The Lord's Prayer is often mumbled
or simply repeated mechanically, but if we really
mean the words we say, this prayer is a great affir-
mation of faith.

Actually Christianity is a gamble, indeed the
greatest gamble in the world. We put our whole life
in the balance, we risk all on our belief that there is
a God and that he cares for us. To call this invisible,
intangible God "Father" represents a great step into
the darkness.

And yet if we have known God through his Son
Jesus Christ, there is nothing more sure in the
world than the existence and the love and concern
of God. If we have sung, as many do at the time of
confirmation: "O take my hand, dear Father, and
lead thou me," then we hallow God's name each day
as we walk through this world, guided by the invisible but real God.

*Thy*
*kingdom*
*come.*

**Matthew 6:10a**

| | |
|---|---|
| **DRAMA** | *Thy Kingdom Come* |
| **MEDITATION** | *Let It Come Now* |

# Thy Kingdom Come

## CHARACTERS

GWEN GARDEN: middle-aged, pleasant, but rather intense

JACK GARDEN: Gwen's husband; middle-aged, relaxed, argumentative at times

HENRY MODAN: dressed a bit more formally, although in sports attire; nervous, concerned

## SETTING

The scene is outdoors. No real scenery is needed except three outdoor chairs. A table could stand in stage center, but this is not necessary.

(As the scene opens, JACK is sitting on one of the chairs, staring toward the audience with field glasses. GWEN enters, excited.)

GWEN: Jack — Jack! There's a boat heading for the landing.

JACK: I know, dear. I've been watching it through the glasses for the past 10 minutes.

GWEN: *(Disappointed.)* I might have known. I never get to surprise you. *(Excited again.)* But who do you suppose it is? We don't get many visitors here on the island.

JACK: I don't have to guess. I know. It's Henry Modan.

GWEN: Are you sure?

JACK: It must be Henry. He hasn't been here for almost five months, and that's the longest time he's ever left us alone. *(Lifting glasses again.)* Besides, I can see him clearly through my glasses.

GWEN: *(With light sarcasm.)* Oh, fine. The great detective. Elementary, my dear Watson. Well, I'm glad Henry's coming. You had such a hot discussion last time that I wondered if he would ever come back. *(Sits.)*

JACK: Oh, Gwen! Henry and I understand each other. We argue, but we don't fight.

GWEN: I should hope not. He's almost our only link with the past. But what do you suppose he wants this time?

JACK: The same thing he always wants. He'll come and tell us how bad things are in the world and then he'll scold me for wasting my life on this island. He'll threaten, and then beg me to come back to work again, insisting that humanity can't do without me and that I owe it to everyone to give up this Robinson Crusoe existence and come back to civilization.

GWEN: You really do know him, don't you. You sound exactly like him. But what kind of an answer are you going to give him this time?

JACK: *(Slowly.)* That all depends. Gwen, have you been happy here the past two years, just you and me, living on this island?

GWEN: You know I have. It's been the best two years of our life together. When we were in the city, you were always dashing here and there, attending a conference, conferring with some business people, or interviewing some foundation officials to raise money for a pet cause. I was just a brief stopover between planes.

JACK: Was it that bad?

GWEN: Well, not really. But I felt like you had been chipped into dozens of little pieces and I hadn't gotten my share. Here we've been able to be together all the time, just you and me. It's been heaven.

JACK: That's my word for it too. So your advice is— we stay here?

GWEN: That's right. But I'm ready to do whatever you want. Maybe this is just too boring for you.

JACK: Gwen, I wouldn't exchange even one of these

peaceful days on our island for the chance to be president of the company I worked for. Or president of the United States, for that matter.

GWEN: *(Gaily.)* Well, I guess you're ready for Henry then. Do you think you ought to go down to the dock to meet him?

JACK: No, he knows the way. *(Looks through glasses.)* He's already tied up his boat. Besides, if I go trotting down there, he'll insist that I'm lonely here and just bursting for company. I think we'll let Henry come to us.

GWEN: All right, dear. *(Pause.)* I suppose he'll stay for lunch?

JACK: He's counting on it—although he'll pretend he wasn't even expecting to be asked. What polite liars we all are.

GWEN: I think I hear him on the path now.

JACK: Yes, he's not slowing down any. (HENRY *emerges from opposite side of stage. He may come from the audience side if necessary.*) Henry, what a delightful surprise. *(They shake hands.)* We certainly weren't expecting you.

HENRY: You old liar. I had the glasses on you while you were watching me. *(They poke each other playfully.)* How are you, Gwen? *(Shakes hands with her.)*

GWEN: Couldn't be better. It's so good to see you, Henry. Good to see anyone on the island here.

HENRY: I don't suppose you have many visitors.

JACK: Oh, I don't know. There's an oriole that comes and sits on that tree out there every morning. *(Points to tree.)* And last week we were visited by two raccoons and one skunk. Sometimes the visiting gets to be more than we can stand.

HENRY: The same old Jack.

JACK: Come on, sit down and chat a while before you tell me what you came for. *(They all sit.)*

GWEN: You'll stay for lunch, won't you?

HENRY: For lunch. Oh, I don't want to put you out. I didn't think about staying that long. (JACK *and* GWEN *exchange nods.*) Still, if it isn't any trouble. I do have a lot of things to talk about.

GWEN: Good. We have a freezer, you know. What'll you have, lobster or steak?

HENRY: I didn't know roughing it was quite that rough. Anything, Gwen. But not too fancy. My ulcer has been giving me trouble lately.

JACK: Mine's doing wonderfully. Mainly because I don't have an ulcer.

HENRY: That dig was meant for me. You both *do* look wonderful. This island seems to agree with you.

JACK: It has to. Even the weather doesn't dare disagree with Gwen.

GWEN: Jack! That's an old joke.

JACK: Well, I don't hear any new ones out here. But

speaking of jokes, tell me, Henry, how are things in town?

HENRY: *(Holds head in hands.)* Terrible, just terrible.

JACK: *(Laughs.)* You're your usual optimistic self.

HENRY: There isn't any other word to describe things. They're terrible. Much worse than when you two lived in the city. (JACK *and* GWEN *exchange glances.* HENRY *is running true to form.)*

GWEN: What's happened to make life so much worse?

HENRY: I don't know. People just don't care about anything anymore. Jack, you remember that athletic club we organized on the south side of town? And that community center we finally managed to build and furnish?

JACK: Of course I remember it. We begged money for the building from almost every "outstanding" citizen in town. Old man McDavis almost had a heart attack when we told him how much we wanted from him.

HENRY: *(Bitterly.)* He should have saved his money. They all should have.

GWEN: What happened? Did the place burn down?

HENRY: Worse than that. It fell apart. Vandals got in and broke up all the equipment. Then some teenage gangs got busy and finished the job. There's nothing left but four crumbling walls now.

GWEN: Why, that's awful!

JACK: It sure is. I put a lot of sweat and prayers into that building. Couldn't you have done something to fix things up again?

HENRY: Oh yes. The building was insured. We could have rebuilt it, but everyone felt it wasn't worth the effort. That's just a sample of what's happening out in the world. But worse than a building being destroyed is what's taking place in the lives of people. There's dope in the schools, even down to the third grade now. Kindergarten kids will soon bring their pills and syringes to class on opening day. And we've got more young alcoholics than we had winos when you were there. And the crooks are back in city hall again. We ran them out with our clean government campaign, but they're in charge of things again and robbing the people, per usual.

JACK: All that in two years. I guess it's true that good people get tired of being good before bad people get tired of being bad.

HENRY: Nobody will argue that point with you. Especially me.

GWEN: *(Stands up.)* Look, while you two sit here and cheer each other up, I think I'll go in and start lunch, OK?

JACK: OK.

HENRY: Yes, Gwen. I've got some things I want to talk to Jack about—just for his ears.

JACK: *(Aside.)* I'll tell you all about it later, dear.

(GWEN *exits.*) You do spread a bit of gloom when you come, Henry. Now I suppose you're ready for your big pitch.

HENRY: What big pitch?

JACK: You know what I mean. After you're finished telling me how bad things are, you're going to tell me I ought to move back into the city and help you and the rest of the do-gooders, aren't you?

HENRY: Why do you think I would do a thing like that?

JACK: Oh Henry, stop being coy. For the past two years you've come out here every three or four months and tried to coax me into going back into town and working with you to clean up all the messes that people make for themselves. Why should this time be any different?

HENRY: I guess I deserve your suspicions. I *have* tried to get you to come back to work with me. But this time it's different.

JACK: Oh yeah! Then what made you come today? Just the desire to see me and Gwen? It's flattering if that's why you made the long trip to this remote island. But I doubt if that's the only reason for your being here.

HENRY: You always were a suspicious man, Jack Garden. All right, I do have a special reason for coming today. But first, I need to know the answer to one question. (*Gets up.*) We've always been good friends, Jack, and I want you to level with me today as friend to friend.

JACK: All right. You really sound serious.

HENRY: I am. Jack, why did you decide to leave your job as an architect and abandon all the projects you and I were working on and move to this remote island?

JACK: *(A bit stunned. He hadn't expected this.)* Well, let's just say I got tired of the rat race I was running.

HENRY: Let's say there's something more than that. Level with me, Jack. I remember how sudden your decision was. On Friday you were busy helping me plan the United Way appeal. And on Monday you were ready to quit your business and move someplace far away. You left me holding the bag on that appeal. I don't mind that, but I've got to know why you made your decision.

JACK: Henry, I've never told a soul, not even Gwen, what made me change so suddenly. And it's hard to tell you, because you may not believe me. But if you must know, I made my decision after listening to a guest preacher at our church Sunday morning.

HENRY: *(Astonished.)* You gave up your business and moved out here because of something a preacher said?

JACK: Don't sound so overwhelmed. I know, even

preachers don't believe people listen to their sermons anymore. And maybe most of us don't listen every Sunday. But now and then the person in the pulpit says something that sticks and stuns. That's what happened to me. That visiting preacher shook my whole world apart.

HENRY: Wow! That must have been a moving sermon.

JACK: It was. It moved me 300 miles away from the city.

HENRY: Well, for heaven's sake, what did the man say?

JACK: Patience, patience. Remember your ulcer, Henry. *(Henry sits.)* You know how we used to talk about making the world a better place to live in, about how we were workers building the kingdom of God? We always opened any committee meeting with prayer and we talked about being light and salt in the world.

HENRY: Yes, of course we did, and why not? We tried to put a religious emphasis on everything we did for the community. Are you saying we were hypocrites and you suddenly found it out?

JACK: Nothing of the kind. We weren't hypocrites. We were fools. You see, this preacher was talking about the kingdom of God too, just the way we did. Only he said human beings couldn't build the kingdom. It comes from God. It's *his* kingdom and he alone can bring it about. All we can do is wait for God to act.

HENRY: And you decided to wait for him here? Is that it?

JACK: Yes. Partly. Only there was more in the sermon. The preacher was one of those fellows who like to talk about sin. Most preachers do, I guess. But he insisted that sin was something you can't get away from. It's in everybody and it never leaves us while we're on this earth.

HENRY: I can believe that. Especially after seeing what happened to that community center.

JACK: I suppose I had always known what that preacher was saying. But suddenly it hit me. You and I were simply trying to hold back the ocean like that old Danish king, Canute. We were trying to make people better and reform the world, and the world wasn't having any of it.

HENRY: And you called me a spreader of gloom! But Jack, maybe you misunderstood what the man was saying. Did he really say we should give up trying?

JACK: No, he didn't say that. But what he did say sounded like the truth to me. At least it was what I wanted to hear. And if he was right I'd been a fool, trying to make God's kingdom come on earth and trying to drive the sin out of people when it can't be driven out. When I saw that, I just decided to give up.

HENRY: Give up? Give up what?

JACK: Give up being a fool. I was a do-gooder who had learned he was a failure. And what you've been telling me this morning shows I was right in coming here. People don't get any better. The crooked politicians creep back. The kids only find new ways to get into trouble. The kingdom of God isn't any nearer than it was when Jesus first talked about it. If this world is going to be changed, God's got to do it. That's what we pray for, isn't it—*"Thy kingdom come."* Am I right?

HENRY: I wish I could say no. But I can't.

JACK: Of course you can't. And that's why I'm here on the island and not dragging out my life in the city. Look, Henry, every morning while you're fighting traffic to get down to your office, Gwen and I can sit here and listen to the birds singing in those magnificent trees out there. *(Gestures.)* All day long while people are snarling in your ear, we can relax here and watch the light play on the water. It's different each day, but it's always beautiful. And when the night comes and you have to be afraid of your own shadow in the city, we can look into the woods and listen to the hoot of an owl or glimpse the night animals slipping through the darkness for food or companionship. Henry, if I could, I'd talk you into coming here instead of your getting me to return to the city. It's heaven here. It's a little taste of that kingdom before it arrives.

HENRY: *(Stands up.)* You don't have to sell me on

your island paradise, Jack. I've already sold myself.

JACK: What do you mean?

HENRY: Simply that for the past few months I've begun to think you've been right and I've been wrong all along. The world *is* dirty and ugly and the people in it are *impossible.* I'm thinking of moving out here, close to you.

JACK: I don't believe it!

HENRY: You'll have to believe it. I stopped on the way here and inquired about some land at the other end of this lake. I told the owner I might be back later this afternoon and take an option on the property. And what you've just said has convinced me. I'm through beating my brains out against a brick wall. Civilization can get along without me. It's going to have to.

JACK: But that's wonderful. We'll sure be glad to have you close to us. (*Stands and shakes hands with* HENRY. *Then calls.*) Gwen — Gwen! Wonderful news! Come out here a minute.

GWEN: (*Wearing an apron.*) What's the matter? Ten handsome pirates attacking the island? Where are they?

JACK: No, silly. Henry's got some wonderful news for us. (*Pokes* HENRY.) You old rascal. You let me think all the time that you wanted to get me back into that rat race.

HENRY: That was all in your mind, not mine.

GWEN: Will somebody please tell me what the wonderful news is?

JACK: Tell her, Henry. You should have the honor.

GWEN: Well, somebody better tell me or there isn't going to be any lunch. I'm going on strike.

HENRY: It's very simple, Gwen. For the past two years I've nagged at you two for coming out here and living on this island. Guess I was jealous, more than anything else. But I've decided to move out here too. I'm looking at some property at the other end of the lake.

JACK: Can you imagine that, honey? We'll see old Henry almost every day. It's wonderful news.

GWEN: *(Slowly.)* I think it's terrible.

JACK: What!

HENRY: Gwen, I promise not to make a nuisance of myself.

GWEN: Oh, it's not that. I didn't mean it that way.

JACK: *(Angry.)* Well, I think you better explain what you did mean.

GWEN: All right. Look, Jack, before Henry came you asked me if I was happy here.

JACK: And you said you were.

GWEN: Yes. And one of the reasons I was happy was that Henry was still living in the city.

JACK: This sounds like a Grade B movie. Now please explain what *that* means.

GWEN: I will if you'll give me time. I felt badly when we ran away from town and left everyone else to deal with the problems there. Christian people should learn to face life where they are. But I consoled myself by thinking that Henry was still there working and trying to make things better for others. But if he comes here, then we've got to go back. Somebody's got to care.

JACK: Look, dear, I've just been explaining to Henry. Now I'll have to repeat it to you. It's not a question of caring or not caring. It's just that we can't do anything about the world and its ugliness. God has to change things and he'll only do that when he's ready.

GWEN: I know that. It doesn't change the fact that we have to care for people.

HENRY: But Gwen, if we really can't make the world over, what's the use of trying?

GWEN: Because, my two bright theologians, we've got God dwelling inside of us. That's his kingdom now. But he'll only stay there if we show concern for others. He wants us to love *people,* not just squirrels and sunsets.

JACK: Gwen, you're forgetting one thing—sin. The world is full of evil and it doesn't get any better. There are more evil people in the world today than there were when Jesus was here. It's a losing fight.

GWEN: Henry, do you remember Mike, the freckle-faced boy who came to the community house you and Jack built?

HENRY: Of course I remember him. Meanest kid we ever had in that community program.

GWEN: What's he doing now?

HENRY: Why, he got a scholarship and he's in college now. Doing very well, I believe. He certainly straightened out, although it was a tough struggle.

GWEN: OK. Now Jack, I'd like to remind you of Mildred, that young woman who was your secretary for a while. Can you think of anything unusual about her?

JACK: Oh, you know as well as I do that she spent two years in prison before she came to work for me. I took her on out of pity, I suppose. But she was the best secretary I ever had.

GWEN: All right. I could go on and on. But I rest my case right now.

HENRY: *(Slowly.)* I see what you're driving at. You're saying the amount of sin may not change but some of the sinners do.

GWEN: Exactly. That kingdom of God you two have been talking about includes individuals as well as some grand change at the end of the world. And while we're here in this life, we may not win everybody for Christ, but with his power, some lives are changed.

JACK: But Gwen —

HENRY: You're right, of course. You put things clearer than Jack did. I suppose I was just discouraged when I came out here. It's so easy to remember the defeats and to forget God's victories. *(Pause.)* I guess I won't stop and see that real estate man after all.

JACK: What are you saying?

HENRY: Simply that I still can't go for your way of life, Jack. I thought I could, but Gwen's knocked the props out from under me. I can't run away from the world, even though this spot seems ideal. And I'm not worrying about God's kingdom anymore. It can come when he's ready for it, but until it does, I've got to keep on fighting where the battle is hot.

GWEN: Good, good! *(She looks at JACK, who reads her meaning.)*

JACK: Gwen, you're an angel—or a devil.

GWEN: I said I was ready to do whatever you wanted me to do. I'm not asking you to do anything.

JACK: Not much! You know I've been happy here with you. But I suppose you have also suspected that back in my mind was the question: Have I made the right decision? Can I run away from people?

GWEN: We can always have this place to come to when we need a rest. Everyone needs some time to themselves.

JACK: Then you know my decision. Henry, this time

you get your wish. I'm coming back to town with you.

HENRY: But I didn't even ask you.

JACK: No, but God did. *(Looks at* GWEN.*)* Through a little messenger. I guess if I'm going to be in his kingdom, I'd better be a worker, not just a spectator.

# Let It Come Now

"Thy kingdom come."

The first Christians had a very simple view of life. They believed that in a few short years Jesus was going to return to them as a triumphant king, ruling over the earth. In fact, just 40 days after the resurrection, the disciples asked: "Lord, will you at this time restore the kingdom to Israel?" (Acts 1:6). Because they were so sure of what the future held, when those early believers prayed, "Thy kingdom come," they felt they were talking about an event that was just around the corner.

Today we are some 1900 years away from that first generation of Christians, and the kingdom is yet to come. Although people in almost every age have said the end is near, they have all been disappointed. The Lord has not returned to set up his kingdom. Today people are once again telling us that these are the last days, and of course they may be right. But what do we mean when we pray together: "Thy kingdom come?" Have the words lost their meaning, since Jesus hasn't returned?

Not at all. We are still hoping and longing for Jesus to return and to set up God's reign on this earth. We may not express our hopes in precisely that way, but we are all longing for a better world. Aren't we all tired of wars and rumors of wars? Aren't we all tired of crooked politicians and of business executives who lie about their products? Aren't we sick of sickness and wearied to death of death that robs us of our loved ones?

Human beings have always dreamed of a better world, a world freed of its imperfections. Paul even says that all of creation groans for release from the effects of sin. And that universal longing is expressed in the Lord's Prayer by the simple words, "Thy kingdom come." When we say that petition we are expressing a desire for Christ to return and to set up his kingdom.

It is important that we never lose sight of that promise, that dream. Sometimes this world gets too comfortable and we settle down in it, content to tolerate the imperfections that disturb us. We say, "Thy kingdom come," but we don't really mean it. We are like the lazy man who stops chasing flies away from himself and just decides to live and let live.

Christians ought never adopt such a passive mood. We have a goal, a promise, and we should long for it every day. We need to feel like the faithful Christian who looked up into the sky each morning and said, "Maybe today, Lord."

In that strange book, Revelation, the writer sees the new Jerusalem coming down from heaven and hears a voice declare: "Behold, the dwelling of God

is with men. He will dwell with them, and they shall
be his people, and God himself will be with them;
he will wipe away every tear from their eyes, and
death shall be no more, neither shall there be mourn-
ing nor crying nor pain any more, for the former
things have passed away" (21:3b, 4).

When we think of a vision like that, it isn't difficult to say, "Thy kingdom come."

However, mere longing for a better world can be
a lazy person's way to face life. There is an old story
of a farmer who said lightning struck an old shed
and thus saved him the trouble of tearing it down,
and rain washed off his car and saved him that chore
too. When asked what he was doing now, he re-
plied, "Waiting for an earthquake to shake the po-
tatoes out of the ground." Nice cooperation if you
can get it—but that's not quite what we mean with
the words, "Thy kingdom come."

Luther said in explaining this petition that we
pray God's kingdom may also come to us. In other
words, even before the end of the world, there is a
sense in which God sets up his kingdom in the hearts
of individual believers. Children love to sing:

> Into my heart, into my heart,
> Come into my heart, Lord Jesus;
> Come in today, come in to stay,
> Come into my heart, Lord Jesus.

That's part of our prayer when we say, "Thy kingdom come." We are asking God to take charge of our
lives. We want him to be our king. And we want
that to happen now.

Two special truths must be noted here. First, God

will not take charge of our lives as a result of our efforts. Just as the return of Jesus is in God's hands, not ours, so his coming to us is an act of grace. We don't fulfill this petition ourselves by pious prayers or good deeds.

People like to talk about "getting right with God," as though this were something that human beings can do. But that's all wrong. God comes into our hearts through his own will. The initiative is his. We are simply saying that we are ready for him to come when we pray the Lord's Prayer.

Yet the other side of the coin is also true. We can impede or prevent God's action. We can nullify God's good intentions. Perhaps the best picture of this is also from the book of Revelation, where Jesus is pictured as standing at the door of the human heart and knocking. He does not push the door down. God does not force himself on anyone.

So when we pray, "Thy kingdom come," we are indicating our willingness to let God enter and take charge of our lives. We are saying, "Let it come now for me. The door is open, God. Come in and fill my life." So, whether Christ delays his coming for another 2000 years or returns tomorrow, we can still pray for his kingdom to come now, to us.

*Thy will be done,*
*On earth*
*as it is in heaven.*

**Matthew 6:10b**

| DRAMA | *Thy Will Be Done* |
|---|---|
| MEDITATION | *Who Does the Work?* |

# Thy Will Be Done

## CHARACTERS

PROFESSOR GEORGE MITCHELL: professorial type, rather dry in delivery

BARBIE MCIVER: teenager or early 20s

MOTHER: a bit loud, argumentative

CHUCK MCIVER: teenager

FATHER: inclined to be bossy

## SETTING

The scene is a typical living room, with few chairs, only one of which is really necessary since the characters do not sit down, although they may do so at the end.

(As the scene opens, PROFESSOR MITCHELL is standing at a podium outside the stage area. He does not appear on stage during the play but must be in a prominent place so he can be seen.)

MITCHELL: Good evening, ladies and gentlemen. Permit me to introduce myself. I am Dr. Mitchell, Dr. George Mitchell from the State University. I am the head of the Department of Sociology there. My lecture tonight will concern the subject of human conflict and its consequences.

Now as we all know, conflict is a common problem in our modern society. We find conflict in the home, in politics, in business, and even between nations. What we don't always understand is what causes these struggles. So to help you comprehend how trouble arises and also to suggest some simple solutions, I have brought with me tonight some actors from our university. They have been giving these demonstrations wherever I have been lecturing, and I think you will find their presentations interesting.

Let us begin by looking into an average home and seeing what happens between Joan McIver and her daughter, Barbie. *(Turns to stage.)* Actors, the stage is yours.

BARBIE: *(Comes on stage and searches around frantically. Finally she calls offstage.)* Mom, Mom, have you seen my purse?

MOTHER: *(Hurries on stage.)* Barbie, you'd lose your head if it weren't fastened on. Have you looked behind that green chair? That's where you usually leave your things.

BARBIE: *(Discovers purse.)* Oh yes, here it is. Thanks, Mom. What would I do without you?

MOTHER: Sometimes I wish you'd try for a week or two. *(Suspiciously.)* But what's all the hurry about finding your purse? You don't need it until tomorrow, do you?

BARBIE: I happen to have a date tonight.

MOTHER: You didn't tell me you had a date.

BARBIE: Well, I think I'm old enough to come and go as I please without signing in and out.

MOTHER: Don't take that tone of voice with me, young lady. I suppose you're going out with that James Webster again.

BARBIE: And what if I am?

MOTHER: You know I don't like him. Your father doesn't like him. Even your brother doesn't like him.

BARBIE: Well, that's just too bad. But you see, none of you are going to marry him so your opinions don't make any difference.

MOTHER: And neither are you going to marry him! I won't have you throwing your life away on that good-for-nothing.

BARBIE: It may interest you to know that he hasn't even asked me to marry him.

MOTHER: And what if he does!

BARBIE: *(Maddeningly.)* Then—then—then—I'll make up my mind. But you're not helping matters with your nagging and criticism.

MOTHER: Oh, so I can't even talk to you any more. *(Pause.)* I'm only doing it for your own good.

BARBIE: My good doesn't have anything to do with it. You simply want to run my life and tell me what to do, just like I was a little kid.

MOTHER: You're the one who's being stubborn. You want your own way and you don't care who you hurt as long as you can do what you please.

MITCHELL: *(Snaps fingers. The actors freeze in their positions and remain in place during the following speech.)* We'll stop our drama right here for a moment. Sounds familiar, doesn't it? In one form or another this kind of conflict is probably going on right now in thousands of homes. And it's all a contest of wills. The mother thinks she is acting in the best interest of her daughter. But really she sees in the young man a threat to her control over her child. If once Barbie marries and leaves home, the mother will have lost her dominance forever. So she fights and argues, determined that her own will must prevail.

But the daughter also has a will. She probably isn't as serious about the young man as she seems to be. But all her life she has felt dominated by the mother. Now she's grown up. She wants to be able to come and go as she pleases. She wants to be able to make her own decisions. And so the clash of wills occurs, for each character is bent on having her own way.

Now let's bring a third person on stage—that brother that the mother referred to. Notice what happens now in the battle of wills. *(Snaps fingers and the characters resume animation.* CHUCK *comes on stage.)*

CHUCK: Say, what's all the hollering about? I could hear you two upstairs. You were drowning out my stereo.

BARBIE: That'll be the day. You were probably down here listening at the keyhole.

MOTHER: *(Primly.)* Barbie and I were having a private discussion.

CHUCK: Private! The whole neighborhood was probably tuned in. I'll bet you two were arguing over that nutty Jim Webster.

BARBIE: *(Haughtily.)* That's none of your affair, Chuck McIver.

CHUCK: Oh, no! All the guys at school keep asking me, "Is your sister going to marry that old nutty Jim Webster?" It makes me mad.

BARBIE: I'll thank your friends to keep out of my affairs.

MOTHER: You see, Barbie. Everybody knows what that boy is like. I don't see why you can't see through him.

BARBIE: I might have known. Now you're going to gang up on me. Just like you always do.

MOTHER: What do you mean by that?

CHUCK: Yeah. Who's ganging up on you?

BARBIE: You and mother. Ever since you came

around this house, Chuck McIver, it's been you and mother against me.

CHUCK: That's not the way I see it.

BARBIE: Well, that's the way it is and always has been. When you were little, I had to mind, while you could get away with murder. *(Sarcastic.)* You were the baby. And when you got older, you could do things because you were a boy and I was only a girl. It's always been like that. You've been the favorite and I've been the step-child.

MOTHER: I'm sure your father and I have tried to treat you both as you deserved. In fact, better than you deserved in most cases. And I don't think we ought to continue this discussion.

CHUCK: Oh, no. You're not cutting me off until I have my say. *(To Barbie.)* What do you mean, I've always been the favorite? You don't know what it's like to be told you're too young to do what your sister is doing. You don't know what it's like to grow up being Barbie's little brother. The school teachers all keep reminding me of the good grades *you* got in school. That makes me feel like the family idiot. You don't know what it's like to have your sister drive you to parties because you're too young to drive. And you got to spend your vacation at that fancy summer camp and I didn't even get to go because we didn't have enough money when my turn came. I think the shoe's on the other foot. You're the favorite. I get what's left.

MOTHER: Now children, I don't like to see you fighting like this.

BARBIE: Well, tell him to butt out of my business.

CHUCK: That's right. Butt out. I'm plenty helpful when you want something done, but if you don't like what I say, I'm supposed to butt out. I'm sick of this family.

MITCHELL: *(Snaps fingers again and the actors freeze.)* Suppose we stop our actors again and analyze what we just heard. In this scene we had sibling rivalry clearly demonstrated. Children in a household are natural competitors for attention from their parents and others. And because each child wants to have his or her own way in everything, bitter quarrels often break out. Little birds in their nests *don't* agree, despite the poem which says they do, and children aren't any more peaceable toward one another.

And, of course, as the conflict rages between the children, parents are drawn into the struggle and may play favorites or at least seem to do so. So instead of being a place of tolerance and compromise, many a household resembles a battlefield with sniping and quarreling going on almost continually.

But we have one more character to introduce into our drama—the father. Let's bring him on stage and see how the tides of conflict shift and swirl around him. *(Snaps fingers. Cast comes to life.)*

FATHER: *(Enters.)* What's all the noise about? Can't

a man have a little peace and quiet in his own home?

CHUCK: It's Barbie.

MOTHER: It's these kids.

BARBIE: It's mother. *(The three speeches are almost said together.)*

FATHER: One at a time, please. Joan, what's the argument about this time?

MOTHER: We were just having a little discussion about Barbie and that Webster boy.

CHUCK: Yeah, old nutty Jim Webster.

BARBIE: Why you—*(Takes after* CHUCK. FATHER *catches her and pulls her back into her place.)*

FATHER: Stop it, you two. *(They stand facing him.)* Now look. I don't want to hear any more on this subject tonight. We discuss Jim Webster almost every day in this house. And I'm getting sick of it.

BARBIE: *(Sees her advantage.)* That's right, daddy. You tell them to be quiet. It's nobody's business except Jim's and mine.

FATHER: I didn't say that. I don't like him and I wish you'd stop seeing him. But he isn't much worse than the rest of the boys you run around with. All of them have long hair and wear dirty clothes. I don't know how you stand any of them. *(Walks as he says this. Turns stage left.)*

BARBIE: That's the trouble with this family. You're all back in the dark ages.

CHUCK: That's the first sensible thing you've said to-night, sis.

FATHER: Is that so! Well, maybe the dark ages weren't so dark then. Anyway, I don't want to hear anymore about anything tonight. I just want to read my paper and watch a little TV.

CHUCK: Boy, free speech doesn't stand a chance around this house!

MOTHER: Now Chuck, you shouldn't talk like that to your father. You should show more respect.

CHUCK: Why? Why does father have the right to yell at us, but when we yell back, we're not showing respect?

MOTHER: Because he's your father.

CHUCK: Might know. When the chips are down, it's parents versus kids every time, and we don't have a chance.

FATHER *(Sarcastically.)* I feel sorry for you two. I really do. Why when I was your age—

BARBIE: Oh, my. Here it comes again.

MITCHELL: *(Snaps fingers and the characters freeze again.)* We'll spare you Mr. McIver's reminiscences about his youth. But it's not hard to see what motivates the father in this story. He wants peace and quiet in the household—at his own price. He wants a home where everyone is agreeable and obedient to the father's will. Of course, the day of the dictatorial tyrant is gone in most

families, but that doesn't keep many from longing for the so-called good old days when father's
word was law.

So you see we have explored the problem
faced by all members of the family, and in every
case the cause is the same. Each one wants his
or her will to be supreme. And of course, what
is true in a household is true in every area of
life. The businessman wants *his* plans for the
company to be adopted, the politician wants *his*
laws enacted, the nations of the world want
*their* national ambitions to succeed. And of
course there is no way two or more conflicting
wills can both win out.

That suggests our answer to the conflict of
wills in this world. Life would be much simpler
for everyone if we all learned to give a little, if
we were all willing to compromise, willing to try
to see and understand the other person's view-
point.

CHUCK: (*Snaps out of freeze. Other actors stay fro-
zen.*) Dr. Mitchell, we have another solution to
your problems.

MITCHELL: What! *You* have something to suggest?
But you're only an actor. What do you know
about conflict and its cure? I'm the head of the
Sociology Department, and I've made a special
study of this subject.

CHUCK: Nevertheless, we have a solution to present
to these people today. And we think it's better
than your "Give a little, compromise a little"
idea.

MITCHELL: Well! This is the strangest thing I've ever heard. Are you serious?

MOTHER: Please sit down, Doctor.

BARBIE: I think you'll like this.

MITCHELL: But . . . but . . .

FATHER: *(Comes close and glares.)* Sit down, Doctor.

MITCHELL: Yes, yes, I will. *(Calls.)* Oh, actors! *(Snaps fingers. Cast comes to life.)* Go ahead if you must.

CHUCK: Thank you. Look, I know dad said we weren't to discuss anything else tonight. But I've got an idea and I'd like to share it with you all.

BARBIE: It must be *some* idea if *you've* had it.

CHUCK: Please—just listen to what I have to say. All of you sit down, and let me talk.

MOTHER: I suppose we should listen to the boy.

FATHER: OK. But make it snappy. The sports news is coming on pretty soon. *(They all sit down except CHUCK.)*

CHUCK: I got my idea when we were praying the Lord's Prayer last night at the dinner table.

MOTHER: We always pray the Lord's Prayer at dinner, Chuck. We've done it all your life. What was so special about last night?

CHUCK: I don't know. But suddenly I really heard some words that I had said a thousand times before. They seemed to jump at me. The words were: "Thy kingdom come, thy will be done, on earth as it is in heaven."

FATHER: Well, you got the words right anyway.

CHUCK: I think I got more than the words right. But first, you know what we've been doing this evening? Each of us has been trying to have our own way about something. We've been wanting *our wills* to be done.

BARBIE: What's wrong with that?

CHUCK: You can see what's wrong with it. We've been fussing and arguing like a pack of wild cats. But if we stopped thinking about *our* wills and started thinking about God's will being done . . . .

BARBIE: What's all this got to do with my dating Jim Webster?

CHUCK: I'm not sure. I'm not trying to say that we can always know the answer to everything. Only we *do* know it's not God's will that we should fight and hate one another. And we get pretty close to that at times.

BARBIE: I don't hate anybody.

CHUCK: No one would believe that if they heard how you talked this evening.

BARBIE: *(Rather ashamed.)* Gee, everybody. Was I that bad?

MOTHER: We were all a little sharp with one another. I'm sorry for what I said.

BARBIE: So am I.

CHUCK: Me too.

FATHER: Guess I'd better join the chorus.

CHUCK: This all sounds good. But it won't be long before we'll be fighting all over again unless we make a real change and let God run this family.

MOTHER: Maybe Chuck's got something there.

FATHER: Sounds reasonable.

CHUCK: I propose we all try to live our lives according to God's will, not our own. Let's start right now.

FATHER: *(Muses.)* God's will, not ours. That *is* what we say in the Lord's Prayer.

BARBIE: I've been saying it for years. Maybe I haven't been listening either. It might make a difference.

CHUCK: Think what would happen if the whole world said those words and really meant them.

FATHER: Hold on there. Let's not take on the whole world right away! But you're suggesting, Chuck, that we all try to let God guide us instead of being concerned about our own selfish wants?

CHUCK: Yes, sir.

FATHER: I see. Hmm. *(Makes up mind.)* All right. I'm willing to give it a try. I'm willing to let God have his way with me if the rest of you will try it too.

BARBIE: Count me in. And I'm sorry I was so mean.

MOTHER: We can all say a lot of "I'm sorrys" to each other. But maybe we'll say them best by giving Chuck's plan a try.

CHUCK: It's not my plan. It's God's. And it's been around a long while. It just needs some people to put it to work. *(Steps out of scene. Other actors freeze.)* All right, Mr. Mitchell. There's *our* solution for your conflict-of-wills lecture.

MITCHELL: Young man, I've been head of the Sociology Department at the State University longer than you've lived on this earth. But maybe an old dog *can* learn new tricks. You've got a head on your shoulders. Your plan just might work. At least, the next time I give this lecture, I'll let *you* finish it. Just the way you did now.

# Who Does the Work?

"Thy will be done, On earth as it is in heaven."

Do you want to know where people are the most obedient, the most careful of their conduct? Try a well-run prison. Do you want to live in a land where crime is kept at a minimum, where people obey the law and even the trains run on time? Choose an efficient dictatorship. Even in such places people's sinful nature may exert itself, but the element of compulsion coupled with punishment can check many evil actions.

Many people want God to be a dictator, a kind of warden running this earth as a prison. They want God to stop wars, to keep criminals from murdering, even to get drunk drivers off the road so they won't kill innocent people. But God does not accept the appointed role of dictator or puppet master.

Note what we pray in the Lord's Prayer: "Thy will be done, on earth as it is in heaven." That last proviso—"as it is in heaven"—makes all the difference in the world. For we are asking that God's will be expressed in a special way. No one imagines that God is a heavenly tyrant forcing all heavenly creatures to obey him whether they want to or not. The angels are always pictured as serving God with joy and enthusiasm. And that's what we are asking for on this earth.

Immediately we might conclude either that we are praying for a miracle or that we are asking God to put an end to this world as we know it, for it is only at the end of time that all things will be completely under God's control. But perhaps we can catch a glimpse of a more immediate goal for our prayer if we look at a few specifics.

Does anybody imagine it is God's will that human beings hate one another and slaughter each other in a war? Does anybody think God wants Arabs and Jews to struggle over a few yards of real estate, or whites and blacks in Africa to oppress or murder one another? Of course not. Even those who have been professional soldiers have universally agreed with General Sherman: "War is hell." And hell isn't part of God's kingdom or his will.

Does anybody believe it is God's will that children be beaten and neglected by their parents, that youngsters grow up hungry and ignorant, that young bodies and minds be warped by neglect and mistreatment? Of course not. Jesus reminds us that children are precious in God's sight and that it is a terrible thing to offend one of God's little ones.

Does anybody believe it is God's will that one-third of the world's people starve while others have too much to eat? Does anyone believe . . . we could go on and on. Evidence of injustice and ugliness is everywhere in this world. Anyplace we look, God's will isn't being done.

But we must note one thing. These are all problems we can do something about. The ills of the world can be corrected by the people who caused them in the first place. Why bother God with all this?

A farmer once prayed, "God, feed the hungry." He was rebuked by his son, who said, "If I had what you have in the barn, I would feed them myself."

There is wisdom in the boy's remark. We cannot bring all the world's troubles to God's door and tell him, "You take care of these things." But at the same time, unless our wills have been brought into harmony with God's will, no real improvement will occur. God must provide the impulse, the guidance, if changes are to be made. This action between God and his people is a rather complicated thing, but perhaps we can find guidelines to help us understand this petition.

1. God will not do anything alone. All human progress is made by human beings. Even the spreading of the gospel, important as it is, must be done by weak, fallible Christians. At creation God put this world in the hands of his people, and he has not taken it back under his control. Men and women must serve as God's agents, or nothing will happen.

2. We cannot do anything alone. Jesus said, "Apart from me you can do nothing" (John 15:5). And perhaps this is the place where most of our high resolves finally flounder. We can see what needs to be done, but somehow our energy fails. Once upon a time the nations of the world renounced war, yet wars continue. Every year conferences all over the world meet

and draw up good resolutions, yet the goals are not achieved. The truth is that we need God's help. We need to say, "Thy will be done."

3. The situation isn't hopeless. In many ways this world is a better world than it was in the past. Superstition and witchcraft have been banished from many areas. Human slavery, once thought inevitable, has almost ceased to exist. Debtors' prisons have been torn down. The low status of women in society has been improved. Progress has been made. Dedicated Christians, truly asking that God's will be done and truly seeking to implement that will, have seen their prayers come true.

Someone once said that we must pray to God as if it all depended on him, and we must work as if it all depends on us. That's a good description of what we must mean when we say, "Thy will be done, on earth as it is in heaven."

*Give us this day our daily bread.*

**Matthew 6:11**

| | |
|---|---|
| DRAMA | *Our Daily Bread* |
| MEDITATION | *God and Time* |

# Our Daily Bread

## CHARACTERS

MARTA: a secretary in heaven, inclined to meddle

WALLO: young man; a messenger angel, like a postman

CORAL: older than Marta, rather self-important

PAT: new arrival from earth; male or female

DARCI: commissioner in heaven; tolerant and wise; male or female

(If Pat and Darci are played by women, other characters will say *she*, *her*, and *hers* instead of *he*, *him*, and *his* when referring to them.)

## SETTING

The scene is a small office with at least three chairs and a desk or table.

## COSTUMES

No effort should be made to design special costumes for the characters. MARTA should wear something flashy, CORAL a rather colorful outfit but more subdued than Marta's.

(As the scene opens, MARTA is glancing idly through some papers. Finally she puts them all aside and sits, humming to herself. There is a knock at the door.)

MARTA: Come in. (WALLO *enters.* MARTA *stands up.* WALLO *is loaded down with letters, papers, etc. and may carry a sack like a mailman's.*) Oh, it's you, Wallo. What have you brought me today?

WALLO: The usual. In more than the usual amounts. I've got prayers, petitions, complaints, objections —you name it. This stuff keeps pouring into the prayer reception room.

MARTA: (*Sees the pile and sighs.*) Put it over there on the table. Use one of the chairs if you need to. I thought Coral was taking care of all the complaints.

WALLO: (*Unloads all his bundles.*) I don't know anything about that. I just bring the stuff up here. But we seem to get more begging prayers every day. Somebody must be falling down on the job.

MARTA: But that's not possible here. Everything in heaven is perfect.

WALLO: (*Rather cynically.*) That's supposed to be the idea. But these complaints are real, not make-believe.

MARTA: Well, don't look at me. This office isn't at fault, let me tell you. We only sort out the prayers here and then pass them on to the proper departments. Most of them go to the Office of Supply, and Coral's in charge there.

WALLO: (*Teasingly.*) Somewhere I've heard you're not the fastest file clerk in heaven. Maybe the stuff gets buried in this office and never reaches Coral.

MARTA: *(Defensively.)* That's not fair. I may get a little behind in my filing sometimes, because I have to take charge of most of the affairs of heaven.

WALLO: *(Laughs.)* Oh, Marta, who are you trying to fool?

MARTA: It's true. Darci is one of the high commissioners of heaven and I work for him and advise him. We discuss everything that goes on in the universe.

WALLO: *(Teasingly.)* From the way I hear it, he has to spend half his time getting out of trouble because you interfere in his affairs. Any truth in that?

MARTA: *(Reluctantly.)* Maybe a little. I've had a few setbacks. But I do the best I can. And I certainly manage to get all the prayers into Coral's hands in time for her to take care of people's needs. So don't blame me for what's happening.

WALLO: I'm not blaming anyone. All I know is I'm supposed to bring all the prayers straight to your office for processing. And I have no doubt you and Coral will find some explanation for these complaints. You two will give the whole business a heavenly coat of whitewash.

MARTA: Is that so! Sit down, Wallo, and let me explain how all this business works.

WALLO: Don't explain it to me. I'm just a messenger, and my opinion doesn't count around here. Besides, I'm only repeating what others are saying.

MARTA: *(Shocked.)* You mean people are criticizing me for the way I'm handling the prayers from that miserable little planet?

WALLO: That's what's happening, Marta. Remember the Son has a special interest in the people on earth, and when he was there he told the inhabitants to pray for all their needs. *(Thinks.)* Let's see, how did he put it in that prayer that those people keep saying — "Give us this day . . . this day. . . ."

MARTA: Oh, for goodness sake! He said, "Give us this day our daily bread." But he wasn't telling them just to pray for bread. He meant food and clothing and houses and all the things people need to live on that bothersome place, the earth.

WALLO: I understand that. But if you'll take time to read a few of those prayers and complaints *(Indicates piles of letters.)* you'll find out in a hurry that some people aren't getting enough *bread* to eat, much less anything else.

MARTA: *(Angry.)* Some of those people on earth don't deserve anything. They're sinners and ungrateful wretches.

WALLO: Maybe so, but the Holy One loves those people down there. That's why he sent the Son to earth a long while ago.

MARTA: You don't need to tell me that. I got in trouble for trying to prevent the Son from going. But if people are criticizing me about the way I handle the prayers from down there, something's got to be done. I've got to get to the bottom of this.

WALLO: Oh-oh, I don't like that look in your eyes. They tell me that when you go into action, the pearly gates start to tremble.

MARTA: Don't be funny, Wallo. But now I need your help.

WALLO: *(Scared.)* Don't get me involved in your wild schemes.

MARTA: I'm not thinking up any wild schemes. I just want you to go over to the Office of Supply and tell Coral she's wanted in Darci's office.

WALLO: But Darci isn't here. He's at a meeting of the commissioners of heaven. I saw him there just a little while ago.

MARTA: I know. That's just the point. Coral and I can settle this matter between us without Darci ever knowing anything about it. But if I ask Coral to come over here, she won't come.

WALLO: Oho! She's heard about your schemes too.

MARTA: Well, maybe. Anyway, if you tell her she's wanted in Darci's office, she'll be here right away.

WALLO: *(Reluctantly.)* That doesn't seem quite honest to me.

MARTA: *(Very persuasively.)* Now look, you want to find the answer to all these complaints, don't you? If we can figure out what's wrong and correct it, you won't have to come here every day lugging those thousands of prayers and petitions.

WALLO: *(Slowly.)* That's true. . . . All right, I'll do it. But if Coral scolds me, I'll tell her *you* gave the orders.

MARTA: Don't worry. You won't get into trouble. I'll protect you.

WALLO: You!

MARTA: Well, Darci will. He won't refuse to help me.

WALLO: All right. I'm off like a comet. But you'd better start reading some of those messages. *(Exit.)*

MARTA: What a clown! Still, maybe I better look at some of these before Coral gets here. Hm. *(Picks up envelope and reads contents.)* Thousands starving in Bangladesh, wherever that is. But it's shocking, anyway. *(Picks up another.)* Hm. People dying of hunger in the streets of Calcutta. "Please help us," it says. A long list of names. How awful! I never really read these messages before. I just filed them. *(Picks up envelope.)* Here's a personal one. *(Reads.)* It's from an old woman in California. "I need some decent clothing so I can go to church. My dresses are all rags." *(Throws letter down.)* That's disgusting. What's the matter with Coral! How can she be so neglectful?

CORAL: *(Appears in doorway.)* Did I hear my name mentioned? Where's Darci, Marta?

MARTA: He's at a commissioners' meeting. Very important, I think.

CORAL: But Wallo said I was wanted in Darci's office.

MARTA: That's right. *I* wanted to see you about some important business.

CORAL: I might have known you'd be up to something. Well, you've seen me. Good day to you. *(Starts to leave.)*

MARTA: *(Catching hold of her.)* Wait. Don't go, Coral. I'll admit I used a little trick to get you here. But something serious is happening right here in heaven. And you and I are involved.

CORAL: Don't get me mixed up in any of your schemes, Marta.

MARTA: *(Very nice.)* No schemes, Coral, dear. Please sit down. Let me move some of those letters out of the way. Wallo just dumped them there. But I've got to talk to you about all these prayers and petitions from the earth. They've got me worried. *(Moves some letters onto the floor.)*

CORAL: All right, Marta, you do sound upset. I'll stay. *(Sits on chair.)* But I don't see why you're disturbed about those prayers. You just file them in order and send them on to me. A little late at times but I do eventually get them.

MARTA: Yes, but something is going wrong. Coral, there are more complaints all the time. People on earth aren't getting their so-called daily bread. They don't have enough to eat. They don't have decent houses or adequate clothing. And you and I are being blamed for all this.

CORAL: *(Shocked.)* We're being blamed. But that's impossible. I'm very careful that the people on earth have more than enough for their needs. I've provided more clothing and food and better housing for them every year. In my office we keep a close record of the earth's population and our supplies increase as the population grows. Sometimes I wish the Holy One had never told them to multiply and replenish the earth. That's one divine command they all seem to keep very faithfully. Almost the only one, I might add.

MARTA: Nevertheless, something is decidedly wrong down there. Look at these letters. *(Extends some to her.)* Famine, people dropping dead of starvation, complaints, prayers for houses, clothes, food—it doesn't add up.

CORAL: I can't understand it. I know my records are correct. There's more than enough of everything for all those people. Say, do you think we ought to get Darci to send us down to earth for a visit? Just to see what's going on?

MARTA: Not a chance. Only guardian angels are allowed on earth. Besides, Darci grounded me after I took my trip to see that new constellation.

CORAL: Grounded you? Why?

MARTA: Well, it's a little embarrassing. Somehow I wandered off course and almost caused a collision between a comet and a newly formed moon that wasn't on my chart. It really wasn't any big thing but to hear Darci tell it, I practically caused a catastrophe in space.

CORAL: You really do live, don't you, Marta. What would heaven be without you?

MARTA: I'm not really anxious to find out. But right now I don't want to be blamed for anything going wrong on the earth. In fact I don't want Darci to know that there's any trouble on that miserable little world.

CORAL: But I don't know what we can do if we keep this all to ourselves. Wouldn't it be better to inform the commissioners and let them conduct an investigation?

MARTA: *(Alarmed.)* No, no, no. That would be the worst thing we could do. We might end up by being demoted to singing in one of the choirs. And that's not much fun, believe me. Let me think. *(Silence.)* Maybe that new arrival from the earth, the one who's working in your office, could give us some idea of what's going wrong down there.

CORAL: You mean Pat? (MARTA *nods.*) But he's just been assigned to work for me. How did you know about him?

MARTA: I make it my business to know what goes on in heaven.

CORAL: *(Upset.)* No doubt about that. Too bad you don't make it your business to keep out of other people's affairs.

MARTA: Is that so! Let me tell you—no, I'm not going to quarrel with you, Coral. We're both in trouble if news about conditions on the earth gets noised about. We can't afford to fight.

CORAL: *(Repentant.)* You're right. I take back what I said. Here, let me call Pat. He just might be of some help. *(Goes to door and calls in a loud voice.)* Pat, Pat Jones. Come here to Darci's office right away.

MARTA: *(Dryly.)* That should bring him.

CORAL: I'm so glad to have him. He's a dear person and he catches on in a hurry.

MARTA: Some of the people on earth are very nice, although I can't stand the place myself. Might be nice to visit, but I wouldn't want to live there.

CORAL: I think I hear Pat coming now. No nasty cracks about the earth. He may still be sensitive about his old home.

MARTA: Don't worry. I'll be the soul of discretion, as usual. (CORAL *groans.*) But let me question him. He may be afraid of you' since you're his boss.

CORAL: He has no reason to be afraid. Still, since you started this whole business, you might as well do the asking. *(Knock on door.)* Come in,

Pat. *(Pat enters.)* You're very prompt. Pat, this is Marta. She works for Darci, one of the high commissioners of heaven.

PAT: *(Bows.)* I'm pleased to meet you, ma'am. *(To Coral.)* Does one say *ma'am* to an angel?

MARTA: Just call me Marta. Please sit down, Pat. *(He looks at CORAL, who gives him a sign to sit.)* Tell me, before you came up here, while you were still on that miserable planet—I mean, on that delightful place, the earth, did you have plenty to eat, a nice home, and enough clothes?

PAT: Oh yes. There were even times when I had too much to eat and had to go on a diet.

CORAL: Aha, what did I tell you! Those messages and prayers are fakes.

MARTA: Not so fast, Coral. Pat, this office files prayers and complaints from the earth and we're getting a lot more of them than we used to. Look here. *(Shows letters.)* Famine, poor housing, not enough clothes. All kinds of complaints and prayers from that miserable—that lovely place, the earth. How do you explain all these prayers? Is all this true?

CORAL: Yes, Pat, how do you explain it? There's plenty of food on earth, so much that everyone should have enough for their daily bread, as the Son called it. How come people keep praying like this? Who are they trying to fool?

PAT: Are you serious when you ask a question like that?

CORAL: *(Almost shouting.)* Of course I'm serious. You'll soon find out that the office where you're working is in charge of supplies for the earth. And these prayers are making me look bad.

PAT: Don't you really know what happens?

CORAL: No, we don't. But we intend to find out.

MARTA: *(Quietly.)* We're sure you can help us, Pat. We're baffled by it.

PAT: Oh, you poor innocents. But I suppose it's to be expected. Look, it's very simple. Some people on earth take more than their share, and then there isn't enough to go around.

CORAL and MARTA: What!

PAT: It's a matter of greed and sin. I suppose you've at least *heard* those words up here. Didn't you ever read the story of the rich man and Lazarus the beggar, and how the rich man had a banquet every day while Lazarus only got crumbs? That goes on all the time. Human beings try to get as much as they can of everything, and some people get left out. That's all.

CORAL: But surely they wouldn't keep things from those who need them. They wouldn't feast while others starve.

PAT: Oh wouldn't they! If the poor don't have money to buy what they need, they have to do without.

CORAL: So that's what's been happening to my supplies!

MARTA: No wonder we keep getting those prayers and petitions all the time.

PAT: Yes, and you'll continue to get them as long as the earth exists.

MARTA: Another good reason for getting rid of that terrible place.

PAT: Now wait a minute. There are good people there who try to share with others. There just aren't enough of them yet.

MARTA: Something's got to be done right away. Those wicked greedy people must be punished. I'm sure Darci will help us deal with the rich and the selfish. But I must have a plan to deal with the situation. *(Starts to pace.)*

CORAL: Oh no you don't! You keep out of this, Marta. You and I aren't supposed to run the affairs of heaven, much less those on the earth.

MARTA: When I think about those people who are being mistreated on earth, I just see red. I've got to help them. And I'm going to do my best.

CORAL: Unfortunately, your best sometimes turns out to be everybody else's worst. I say we must report what's happening to the commissioners.

MARTA: Look, I'll agree with you this much. We'll talk the whole thing over with Darci first. But right now I'm ready to suggest that heaven blast those miserable earthlings out of the universe. *(Sees PAT.)* Sorry, Pat, I forgot you were here.

PAT: Maybe I should go back to my job. I really don't want to have anything to do with plans to destroy the earth.

CORAL: You're not to go yet, Pat. We may need you to convince Darci of what's going on down there. And maybe you'll be needed to convince Marta not to be so bloodthirsty.

MARTA: Hah! *(Goes to door.)* Darci should be here by now. Those commissioners talk too much at their meetings. *(Listens.)* I think I hear him coming now.

DARCI: *(Enters just as* MARTA *steps back from door.)* Well, looks like I just finished one meeting and stepped into another. Or is this a nectar break?

MARTA: Oh Darci, you're always joking about a "nectar break." We've been having a serious discussion. By the way, you know Coral from supplies. *(They nod.)* And this is Pat, her new helper from earth.

DARCI: Glad to meet you, Pat. *(They shake hands.)*

MARTA: Darci, Coral and I have a problem and we just have to talk it over with you. At least I promised her I would before I took any action.

DARCI: Glad Coral is having a good effect on you, Marta. Does your problem by chance have anything to do with your old enemy, the earth?

MARTA: It has. We've discovered a terrible scandal down there.

DARCI: My dear, the earth specializes in scandals. Don't take my time with such trifles.

CORAL: This isn't a trifle, Darci. It involves heaven too. Look at all those petitions piled up there. *(Indicates mess on the floor.)*

DARCI: I really don't want to look at them. Marta, if you are going to have guests in here, you'll have to keep a neater office.

MARTA: But these just arrived today. And there'll be more of them tomorrow, and the day after that if we don't do something.

DARCI: *(Resigned to his fate.)* All right. Tell me your big scandal.

MARTA: Darci, we found out the reason we get all these prayers for help from earth is that some people and even some nations (PAT *nods.*) take more than their share of things, and the others are left with little or nothing.

CORAL: It's true, Darci. I've been sending them plenty of supplies, but they've been misusing them.

MARTA: I'm ready to ask the Holy One to destroy the whole earth, or at least get rid of the greedy people down there.

CORAL: I don't know what kind of action to suggest. But the commissioners must be told about this. Heaven needs to know what's going on down there.

DARCI: *(Like an indulgent father.)* My dears, heaven

does know. The commissioners have been aware of this from the start. The rich on the earth keep getting richer and the poor are always suffering. And it's been going on since the beginning of time. Isn't that right, Pat?

PAT: Yes sir. At least that's what our history books say.

MARTA: Well, it's got to stop. A thing like that shouldn't be allowed to go on. It's a scandal in heaven as well as on earth.

DARCI: And just how do you propose to change this situation?

MARTA: Well, the simplest way would be for the Holy One to get rid of the whole pestiferous population down there. But I know he won't do that. At least he could make those who have too much give up their surpluses and share with others. That wouldn't be beyond heaven's power, would it?

DARCI: Nothing is beyond the power of the Holy One. But let me remind you that human beings were made in God's image. You cannot make them good by force or you deprive them of their humanity.

MARTA: All right then. At least the people who have too much can be made to suffer for their sins. Can't we give them indigestion, shorten their lives, and bother their consciences?

DARCI: I suspect that punishment is already in effect for many people on earth. Eh, Pat?

PAT: Oh, yes sir.

MARTA: Well, something more has to be done.

DARCI: Something is being done, Marta. It's been going on for many centuries.

MARTA: What? What are you doing?

CORAL: Yes, I'd like to know that too.

DARCI: It's very simple. Human beings who have learned the message of love from the Son are telling others about that love. They're preaching and showing by their actions that it is important to share with the less fortunate. Human beings are learning to live together in God's world.

PAT: I tried to tell them that, sir.

DARCI: I'm sure you did, Pat.

CORAL: But it's so slow. People are still starving, still doing without the bare needs of life.

DARCI: I know. That's the tragedy of the earth. The solutions for their problems have all been provided, but human beings are slow to respond.

MARTA: Can't we speed things up somehow? Maybe we could send someone down there to perform a few miracles to attract their attention and then teach them what they ought to do.

DARCI: May I remind you that the Son himself did that. And they crucified him. There is no real way to change human beings except through slow, patient love.

MARTA: I give up. Patience is not my chief virtue. But at least let's do something about these foolish prayers. *(Points to pile of letters.)* Can't we tell people to stop praying "Give us this day our daily bread"? Can't we tell them we've done all we can for them? They have the means to solve their own problems.

CORAL: I agree. It's hard to know you're doing your best and then be bombarded with prayers and requests for "daily bread."

DARCI: That sounds reasonable, although I'm not sure how we should go about it. What do you think, Pat?

PAT: It's not for me to object to the ideas of heavenly beings.

DARCI: You're a heavenly being now, Pat. Say what you think.

PAT: Then I don't think it would be a good idea. You see, when we say "Give us this day our daily bread," we're not just asking for something. We're reminding ourselves of the source of all the good things of life. Every time I said that prayer it made me realize that no matter how hard I worked, I wouldn't have anything to show for it unless God was good to me. He gives the rain and the sunshine, he makes the seed grow, and he keeps everything alive on earth. Maybe our prayers are a nuisance to heaven, but I think it's better if people on earth keep on acknowledging God's goodness and their dependence on him.

MARTA: Oh Pat, you make me feel ashamed. Earth's prayers aren't a nuisance. If prayer helps to make people feel better on earth, I'll willingly file a thousand times as many prayers as I do now!

DARCI: Young man, this is a red letter day in heaven. Even archangels have tried without success to make Marta feel ashamed for being so impulsive. And you're right, Pat. Men and women on earth must continue to pray, but also continue to share in love with one another. And now, the nectar break is over. (MARTA *waves at him in amusement.*) Let's get back to work.

# God and Time

"Give us this day our daily bread."

God doesn't seem very much concerned about time. He took 400 years to rescue the children of Israel from Egypt. He let them wander 40 years in the wilderness before they entered the promised land. He waited for centuries before he decided to send the Messiah to this world. And human beings have fussed and fumed because God seems so slow in sending Jesus back to this earth to set up the kingdom. Perhaps the explanation lies in the strange passage in 2 Peter: "With the Lord one day is as a thousand years, and a thousand years as one day" (3:8). Time doesn't seem very important to one whose existence stretches from eternity to eternity.

And yet God is very insistent on *our* living a day-to-day existence. He does not want us to think dreamily about time. The children of Israel wandering in the wilderness were given a gift of manna by God, but they were sternly ordered to gather only enough for a single day. Only on Friday could they store up an extra day's supply so they wouldn't have to work on the Sabbath. In the New Testament Jesus emphasized the same truth by telling his followers: "Therefore do not be anxious about tomorrow, for tomorrow will be anxious for itself. Let the day's own trouble be sufficient for the day" (Matt. 6:34). And in the Lord's Prayer we get the same injunction, the same emphasis: "Give us *this day* our daily bread."

Strange, isn't it, that a God who has apparently no sense of time should be so particular about our living one day at a time? If a thousand years are the same as a day to God, wouldn't it make sense for him to give us all we need for a year or for a lifetime? Why should we be on such a tight time schedule?

One of the reasons probably is the uncertainty of human life. God will always be around, but we may not be. We all know that, and yet human beings have a way of forgetting that they are mortal, programmed to die. I once heard a doctor complain rather bitterly that in these days of wonder drugs, people couldn't accept the fact that everyone must die sometime. So they criticized the doctor if death occurs to someone they care about. But perhaps people have always had this attitude toward death. They do not wish to face their mortality.

So the words of the Lord's Prayer serve to remind us of our frailness. Today we need bread. But tomorrow? Who knows what the morrow brings. Life is uncertain and precarious. Even the ordinary actions of life are subject to a terrible veto. Pious people used to say, after declaring what they would do, "God willing." Some even used the Latin words

*Deo volente,* usually abbreviated D.V. We have abandoned that old custom, but perhaps we need to remind ourselves each day that we can only be sure of the present—tomorrow we may not need any daily bread.

But of course there is another reason for the word *daily* in this prayer. Ideally every Christian knows that life is dependent on the goodness of God. The brief poem by Maltbie D. Babcock says it very clearly:

> Back of the loaf is the snowy flour
>> And back of the flour the mill,
> And back of the mill is the wheat and the
>> shower,
>> And the sun and the Father's will.

But somehow we come to take all this for granted. Because we work and make money and buy things in life, we forget it is God who is the ultimate source of all good. We need a daily reminder that we are dependent on him.

The practice of saying grace at the table is rooted in this truth. We may feel like the farmer who looked at his barn full of stores and wanted to pray over it all at once and get it over with. We may even have some sympathy for the man who looked at the meal of leftovers and saw no need to say any prayer because he had blessed all of this before. But prayer at mealtime reminds us constantly of our heavenly Father's care. He doesn't need our prayers and the food doesn't need our prayers, but we need to remind ourselves daily of God's goodness to us.

Perhaps that's the reason Jesus selects for our

prayer the simplest, most basic food of all—bread. If we are dependent each day on God for the bread we eat, how much more do we need to ask him for all the other things of life. In his Small Catechism Luther gives a rather extensive list of human needs: "Daily bread includes everything needed for this life, such as food and clothing, home and property, work and income, a devoted family, an orderly community, good government, favorable weather, peace and health, a good name, and true friends and neighbors." But the point still remains, we ask God for these things today and we must ask for them tomorrow and every day of our existence.

Some have tried to belittle the petition for daily bread, pointing out that we pray first for heavenly things, the hallowing of God's name, and the coming of the kingdom, before getting to the request for daily bread. But isn't it just as logical to see this petition as embedded in the very heart of the Lord's Prayer? It is the center, and perhaps rightly so, for it reminds us of how we live our time here, *day by day*, always dependent on God's goodness.

*Forgive us our debts,*
*as we also have*
*forgiven our debtors.*

Matthew 6:12

| DRAMA | *Forgive Us Our Debts* |
| MEDITATION | *A Deal or a Gift* |

# Forgive Us Our Debts

## CHARACTERS

HERBA: middle-aged, gossipy woman, rather shabbily dressed and yet with a style about her

ELZER: slick, smooth, prosperous looking

ZACCHAEUS: short, well-dressed, trying to be jovial but having difficulty in his new role

SARAH: young, pleasant

## SETTING

The scene is a bare stage, representing the street in front of Zacchaeus' house. If there is no center door, the side exit can represent the door.

HERBA: *(Standing so she can see the doorway. If desired, several can exit from the house at the opening scene, with no dialogue. Finally* ELZER *enters from offstage.)* Elzer. So nice to see you. You remember me? I was at Hiram's party last week and saw you there.

ELZER: Of course I remember you. Everybody knows you, Herba. And I should have known you would be here. You never miss anything scandalous in Jericho, do you? *(Bows to* HERBA.)

HERBA: I should be angry at you for saying that— even if it is true. But I'm too excited about this business with Zacchaeus to waste time getting angry. Elzer, this is the most thrilling thing to happen in Jericho since the walls fell down! *(Pause.)* And that happened a long time ago.

ELZER: I think you're exaggerating a bit, my dear. This will be forgotten within a week.

HERBA: Oh no, it can't be! *(Shrugs her shoulders.)* Anyway, even if it is, it'll be a very exciting week. Just think of it, the chief publican of Jericho making an exhibition of himself. Climbing a tree to see that Galilean prophet!

ELZER: I'll bet old Zacchaeus is as stiff as a board today. He's a little old for such childish tricks.

HERBA: But that's not the half of it. He has publicly admitted he's been a crook. He's giving away half his money to the poor and he's paying back four times the amount he's stolen from the taxpayers. I've been standing here since early morning, watching how many people have been going in and out, collecting money from Zacchaeus.

ELZER: I'll bet it's breaking the old devil's heart. He probably wishes he'd never opened his mouth.

HERBA: I don't know about that. I haven't seen *him*. But the people sure look happy when they come out.

ELZER: Of course they do. Nothing makes people so happy as getting money they didn't expect to receive. You think you're going to get any?

HERBA: Me? Of course not. I've never had anything Zacchaeus could tax. I scrounge in the street for food, and when I can I live off my friends who like to listen to my gossip.

ELZER: If the government put a tax on tongues, you'd be bankrupt in no time.

HERBA: *(Angry.)* Is that so? Well, let me tell you— No, you're not going to get me into an argument. I might miss something. I'm just going to stand here and watch what goes on. It's the sensation of the year — Zacchaeus the publican turning honest. I can't get over it.

ELZER: Herba, you're more gullible than I thought you were.

HERBA: *(Suddenly surprised.)* Gullible? Do you think this was all fixed up between Zacchaeus and that prophet? *(Relishes the thought.)* Oh, that *would* be a story. But it isn't true, is it? It's horrible to imagine that people could be such hypocrites. Do you really believe such a thing?

ELZER: Not me. It was your own ugly mind that suggested such deception. But let me ask you— what did you think of Zacchaeus before all this happened?

HERBA: Why, I thought he was a vicious, mean little man who took advantage of everyone in Jericho. He was a traitor to our people, a tool of the Roman scum.

ELZER: And what do you think of him now?

HERBA: He's a man who's seen the light, who's agreed to change his ways. I think we'll all have to forgive him for everything that's happened up till now. A man's entitled to a second chance.

ELZER: *(Contemptuously.)* Exactly. And he's certainly got it.

HERBA: Are you saying . . .

ELZER: I'm not saying anything. But can you imagine any other way that Zacchaeus could have gotten back into the good graces of the people of Jericho? Do you suppose he could have bought people's goodwill if he had simply gone around bribing everyone? Do you think he could have gotten into the public eye any better than climbing up that sycamore tree while the whole town was watching?

HERBA: You think he planned it all that way? That it was all a trick? But Elzer—the money! This is costing him thousands of shekels.

ELZER: A cheap way to buy public approval. And he's still the tax collector. He can retrieve all his losses in no time. And keep a reputation for honesty while he does it.

HERBA: You're a cynic, Elzer. I love what you're suggesting. It sounds deliciously low. But I don't believe a word of it.

ELZER: Neither do I, my dear. But I intend to find out how sincere our good friend Zacchaeus is in his repentance.

HERBA: Are you going to go in and demand a big payment from Zacchaeus? Oh, Elzer, does he owe you a lot of money?

ELZER: On the contrary.

HERBA: What do you mean, on the contrary?

ELZER: Just that. Zacchaeus doesn't owe me any money. I owe him. Or at least I should.

HERBA: Did you borrow from him? And now you can't pay back?

ELZER: No, my silly Herba. I suppose I might as well tell you. That's the quickest way to make sure everybody in town knows. You see, Zacchaeus has been pretty shrewd in his tax collecting business. He's cheated a lot of people.

HERBA: He certainly has. You have no idea the people who have been in there this morning to collect money from him. Why there's Miltus and Cardo and Amos and—

ELZER: Spare me the details, Herba. That list will

be all over town soon enough. But what Zacchaeus doesn't know is that while he's been cheating all those people, I've been cheating him.

HERBA: You've what?

ELZER: You heard me. I've been cheating him. Oh he's a slick one, all right, but I've been a little slicker. I reckon by now I've managed to hold back almost 500 shekels from him during the past 10 years.

HERBA: 500 shekels! Oh Elzer, that's almost unbelievable.

ELZER: Heh-heh. That's what Zacchaeus will think. But it's true. It's true.

HERBA: But why are you going to tell Zacchaeus that? Won't that just make him angry?

ELZER: Of course it will. I'm certain of that. But if he gets angry, that will prove that his so-called conversion is just a fraud. And I'm sure it is.

HERBA: I don't understand all of this.

ELZER: It's very simple. It's easy for Zacchaeus to feel like a hero now. People are thanking him and praising him for being so repentant, so noble in giving back four times as much as he stole from others. He has a holy glow about him, thinking God has also forgiven him for all his rascality. It's easy to feel happy when you've been forgiven. But forgiving someone else—that's a different matter.

HERBA: I'm beginning to understand. You're going to make Zacchaeus forgive you for the way you've cheated him.

ELZER: If he can. I don't think he'll pass this test, however. Watch and see. I think he'll storm and rage when he begins to count those shekels that I cheated him out of. And it's not just the money either. It'll offend his pride to know I got the better of him. And a pompous little man like Zacchaeus has plenty of pride, believe me.

HERBA: I like you, Elzer. You're a devil.

ELZER: Yes, aren't I? Oh, I'm going to make Zacchaeus stomp and rage. Don't miss it!

HERBA: I wouldn't for the world. Oh, what a story I'm going to have when this is over. *(Doubtful.)* But are you sure Zacchaeus is going to be angry and not forgiving?

ELZER: I guarantee it. *(Noises backstage.)*

HERBA: I hear someone coming. If it's Zacchaeus, please tell him out here how you cheated him. I want to be sure to see and hear what happens.

ELZER: Don't worry. I intend to tell him the truth right in front of his own doorway. I want to be able to run if he takes after me. (ZACCHAEUS *emerges with* SARAH. ZACCHAEUS *has a bag full of money with him.* ELZER *and* HERBA *pull back for a moment.)*

SARAH: Good day to you, Zacchaeus. You have been more than fair to me.

ZACCHAEUS: I hope the money will help a little to make up for the wrong I did you.

SARAH: All that is forgiven. It was a good day for all of us when that Jesus of Nazareth came to Jericho.

ZACCHAEUS: It was the greatest day of my life. Jesus is a great prophet, perhaps even the Messiah.

SARAH: Still, some of the Pharisees weren't too pleased when he came to your house.

ZACCHAEUS: I know, I know. It was a brave thing for him to do. And a blessed thing.

SARAH: Well, good-bye, and God be with you.

ZACCHAEUS: Good-bye to you, Sarah. And thank you for being so forgiving.

SARAH: It's not hard to forgive a man who's turned honest. (*Sees* HERBA *and* ELZER.) Hm, it looks like you have some more—er—customers waiting. (*Exit.* HERBA *and* ELZER *move back to center stage.*)

ZACCHAEUS: (*Peers.*) It's Herba and—and Elzer, isn't it? (*They nod.*) So glad to see you. Won't you come in?

ELZER: No thank you. We'd rather stand out here and talk, if you don't mind.

ZACCHAEUS: Of course. Some people still find it hard to enter the home of a publican. I understand how you feel.

ELZER: It's not that.

HERBA: Not that at all. I'm always glad to go where anyone invites me. But Elzer wanted to speak to you out here.

ZACCHAEUS: Well, no matter. It's pleasant outside today. First, Herba. Dear Herba, do I owe you any money? I don't recall your paying any tax to me except the head tax that everyone has to pay.

HERBA: Zacchaeus, I wish you did owe me money. I wish someone owed me money. But I'm always too poor to have anything worth taxing. You don't owe me the 10th part of a shekel.

ZACCHAEUS: *(Reaches into bag and offers some coins.)* Then, my dear you should take some of the money I've promised to the poor. You need it as much as anyone else.

HERBA: *(Tempted.)* Oh, no, Zacchaeus. You're a good man and I don't want to take advantage of you.

ELZER: *(In her ear.)* Take the money.

HERBA: No. I still have a little pride. I've always lived by my wits—and by the gifts of my friends. I can make out without any help.

ZACCHAEUS: Let me be your friend, then. Here, take some money. *(Extends the bag to her.)*

HERBA: *(Sorely tempted.)* No, no, I'd better not. At least not right now. Talk to Elzer first.

ELZER: Yes, you'd better talk to me. Enough of this. *(Mocks the other two.)* Take it. No, I don't want

to. Take some. Not yet. I've got something to
say more important than this silly nonsense you
two are carrying on.

ZACCHAEUS: I'm sorry, Elzer. I should not keep you
waiting. Have I cheated you in the past, my
friend?

ELZER: I wish I could say you had. I'd like some of
that repayment money—four times the amount
you stole. But you don't owe me anything. On
the contrary . . . .

ZACCHAEUS: What are you saying?

ELZER: I'm saying something different from all your
other visitors this morning. You remember that
I own two farms with a house on each one of
them, don't you Zacchaeus?

ZACCHAEUS: I should know that. I've been out to in-
spect them often enough. Somehow I always
had a feeling that I didn't get *enough* taxes
from you from those two farms.

ELZER: You felt that way, eh. He-he. Well now,
Zacchaeus, did you know that there was a tunnel between those two farm houses?

ZACCHAEUS: *(Suddenly alert.)* A tunnel! I never saw
any tunnel. I always had to walk the long way
around from one farm to the other.

ELZER: *(Pleased with himself.)* Of course you did.
And maybe you'd be interested to know that
while you were checking one farm, my servants
were moving things to the other through the
tunnel.

ZACCHAEUS: *(Realizes what had happened.)* What! What are you saying!

ELZER: You heard me. It was as simple as one, two, three. My money bags, my jewelry, my fine clothes were never in the house when you came to tax me. They were always on the other farm until you went there. Oh, it was a wonderful trick! No wonder you felt you weren't getting enough tax from me. You see, you weren't.

HERBA: Oh Elzer, how clever.

ZACCHAEUS: *(Angrily.)* Clever! That was a dirty trick, Elzer. You cheated me and the government out of a lot of taxes.

ELZER: I'm sure I did. I think it amounted to about 500 shekels over the past 10 years.

HERBA: *(Impressed.)* 500 shekels!

ZACCHAEUS: You're a crook, Elzer. I'll see that you pay for this.

ELZER: Oh no you won't. I have your signed receipt for each year showing that my taxes were paid in full.

ZACCHAEUS: I'll have you before the magistrates for fraud.

ELZER: A lot of good that will do you. Accuse me and I'll deny every word I've said this morning. And no one will believe Herba here if you call on her to testify for you.

HERBA: He's probably right, you know.

ZACCHAEUS: He is, worse luck. The words of a gossip will never be believed. But there's another way. I'll find your tunnel and expose you before the Roman authorities.

ELZER: Try if you want to. But you'll never find that tunnel. And if you dig up my farm everyone will say, "Zachaeus is crazier than we thought. First he climbs trees to talk to a prophet. Now he's digging for tunnels that don't exist."

ZACCHAEUS: You've thought of everything, haven't you?

ELZER: I've tried.

ZACCHAEUS: Then why have you told me this story? What's the point of it all?

ELZER: *(Very piously.)* Very simple, Zacchaeus. Since you've turned over a new leaf, I'm trying to do the same. Now I want your forgiveness.

ZACCHAEUS: Forgiveness! For pulling a cheap trick like that on me! For cheating the government out of 500 shekels, for making others pay more taxes because you managed to cheat your way out of paying yours? A lot of forgiveness you deserve!

ELZER: I didn't say I deserved it. I only asked to be forgiven.

ZACCHAEUS: Well, you'll whistle a long time before I forgive you for such cheating! If there's anything I hate it's a crook and a scoundrel.

ELZER: *(Laughs.)* Ha-ha, just what I expected. You see, Herba, I told you this Zacchaeus is a fraud.

HERBA: *(Defeated.)* I'm afraid you're right. This'll be a sad story to tell in Jericho.

ZACCHAEUS: A fraud! You've got a nerve, calling me a fraud. You and your tunnel.

ELZER: But you *are* a fraud, Zacchaeus. The worst kind—a religious fraud.

ZACCHAEUS: What do you mean?

ELZER: Simply that you were very happy to be forgiven by Jesus and to shine in Jericho as a man who was repentant for all his own cheating and deceits. But it's a different story when you're the one whose been cheated. Now you want every shekel that's due you.

ZACCHAEUS: But this is different. You fooled me. Everyone knows I was the keenest tax collector in the whole district. And you outsmarted me.

ELZER: And that hurts, doesn't it? Oh, it's easy to accept someone else's forgiveness, especially when it's God doing the forgiving. It's a harder thing when you're asked to forgive. Herba, let's be on our way. I've proven my point and you have a good story to tell everyone.

ZACCHAEUS: Good riddance.

HERBA: Just a minute, Elzer. *(He proceeds off stage.)* I've changed my mind, Zacchaeus, I think I'll take some of that money you're giving to the poor. (ZACCHAEUS *gives her money.*) Thank you. After all, I guess people don't change. I'm a poor scavenger. I can't afford to be proud like you. You're the chief tax collector of Jericho, an important man, so you can afford to give me some money. *(Holds out hand for more.)* If you make it enough, I might even make my story a little less vivid when I tell it around the city.

ZACCHAEUS: You can't afford to be proud, and I can. *(Repeating what he heard.)* Thank you for saying that, Herba.

HERBA: Makes you feel important, does it?

ZACCHAEUS: *(Slowly.)* No. It makes me see the truth. *(Calls.)* Elzer, Elzer, come back.

ELZER: *(Reappears.)* You have some more nasty names to call me, Zacchaeus? Or do you think you know where my tunnel is located?

ZACCHAEUS: No, no, my friend. I was wrong to say harsh things about you, wrong to refuse to forgive you for cheating, even if you didn't really feel sorry for what you did. But you must be patient with me. I'm only beginning to learn how to follow Jesus of Nazareth.

ELZER: What are you talking about? What happened here?

ZACCHAEUS: Herba opened my mind. She said she couldn't afford to be proud, while I could. And that's all wrong. I'm a sinner, a sinner who's received the grace of God. I have no cause to be proud or to sit in judgment over others. Nobody has, because we're all sinners. Elzer, I forgive you.

ELZER: This doesn't make any sense to me at all.

ZACCHAEUS: I'm hardly one to be a teacher to others. But this much I know. God has forgiven my cheating and lying. That's what Jesus told me, and I believe it. But I have to be forgiving too, or his forgiveness doesn't mean anything. You were right to call me a fraud, Elzer. I am a fraud unless I'm willing to forgive too. So I do forgive you, Elzer. Here's my hand on it. *(They shake hands.)*

ELZER: I never thought I would live to see this day. If Jesus of Nazareth can change you like this, maybe there is something in his message.

HERBA: I told you this was a great day for Jericho. Now I *really* have a story to tell my friends!

# A Deal or a Gift

"And forgive us our debts,
as we also have forgiven our debtors."

At first glance this part of the Lord's Prayer
seems simple and clear. We must forgive in order to
get forgiveness. God will wipe our slate clean if we
will do the same for others. It's a very open, reasonable transaction. Jesus even related a parable that
seemed to reflect the same truth. A king is pictured
as forgiving a man a large debt, but when the man
refuses to cancel out a small debt for another, he
himself ends up in debtor's prison. Serves him right,
we think. He didn't keep his part of the bargain.

But somehow all this doesn't sound like God. We
have often been told that God loves us and forgives
our sin, not because of anything we do but because
of what Jesus did for us. We have heard again and
again that we are saved by grace and that grace is
*undeserved* kindness. But in the matter of forgiveness, God seems like a shrewd bargainer. "How
much are you willing to forgive?" he asks. "I'll forgive you the same amount. You've got to forgive in

order to receive forgiveness." Is this really the God we know? Or have we misunderstood?

Perhaps we can explain this prayer by a simple illustration. Suppose you start to carry out the garbage from your home. Both hands are occupied with this worthless stuff. But on the way to the garbage can a kind neighbor hails you and offers you a piece of luscious looking chocolate cake. Of course you want the cake. But you can't take it until you have gotten rid of the garbage. This isn't some kind of a swap or deal. It's simply a fact of life—you can't receive a gift if your hands are already full of something else.

This is the way it is with forgiveness. God's willing to forgive. He's always willing. But as long as you are full of hatred or resentment or ill will toward others, you can't receive the forgiveness. Your hands are full.

So we are not making a deal with God when we pray, "Forgive us our trespasses, as we forgive those who trespass against us." We are really saying, "God, I'm ready to receive your forgiveness now. My hands are empty. My heart is open and freed from resentment." Only when we can say that, can God give us his forgiveness.

Leslie Weatherhead, in a sermon on the parable of the unforgiving debtor, tells about visiting a woman member of his church and chancing to mention the name of another member. That brought a terrible reaction. "I won't have that woman in my house," was the reply. Weatherhead comments on this rather sadly, pointing out that the two Christians would expect to spend all eternity together, yet one would not entertain the other in her home. Such an attitude certainly is not in harmony with God's forgiveness. In fact, if our hearts are full of bitterness, there isn't any way God's forgiveness can get to us.

In his parable of the unforgiving debtor, Jesus gives another clue to the meaning of this part of the Lord's Prayer. When others saw the meanness of the man who wouldn't forgive, they reported that fact to the king, because the man's attitude was a poor witness to the good action of the king himself. And this matter of witnessing is an important one. We are called upon to be salt and light in this world. We are to be little Christs to our neighbors. People are to see our good works and glorify our heavenly Father.

But what if they see bitterness and hatred? Such emotions are a poor witness to our faith. The woman in Weatherhead's story was a bad advertisement for her church and her Lord. The early Christians impressed the pagan world with the fact that they loved one another. The world still looks for that kind of witness. Every town is full of people who refuse to forgive. The world takes note of those who forgive, because forgiveness is the evidence of a changed life and a genuine faith.

Let's not fool ourselves. It isn't easy to forgive. Sometimes the wound is deep and the hurt doesn't want to go away. But if we remember how great God's forgiveness is, how eager he is to love us and bless us, the task will be a little easier.

A biographer of Stalin said of the Russian dictator: "Stalin never forgot or forgave an injury done him. He bided his time and in the end, always hit back."

That is the spirit of the world. As Christians we forgive because we know how good God has been to us. When we say, "Forgive us our trespasses, as we forgive those who trespass against us," or "Forgive us our debts, as we also have forgiven our debtors," we come to God with hands and hearts freed of resentment, ready to receive God's blessings.

*And lead us
not into temptation,
But deliver us
from evil.*

**Matthew 6:13**

| | |
|---|---|
| DRAMA | *The Test* |
| MEDITATION | *Into Deeper Waters* |

# The Test

## CHARACTERS

SINGER: young man with dreamy look in eyes; may play guitar or sing unaccompanied

NATHAN: older man; worried look on his face

FIRST TEMPTER: rather dictatorial; man or woman

SECOND TEMPTER: subtle, sounds seductive; man or woman

THIRD TEMPTER: cynical and sneering, man or woman

## SETTING

The scene represents no particular place, as this play is a fantasy. Two chairs or seats are on stage right. Outdoor furniture is best, but isn't essential.

## COSTUMES

NATHAN and SINGER wear ordinary clothes. TEMPTERS should be dressed alike.

(As the scene opens, the SINGER is seated at stage right. As NATHAN enters from the left, the SINGER begins to sing, "Let Me Tell You the Story of Daniel." NATHAN stops and listens.)

Let me tell you the sto - ry of Dan- iel,

Dan - iel in the li - ons' den. Oh, the Lord put

Dan - iel to the test, Let him suf - fer and

then The Lord brought Dan - iel out of the pit,

Sound of bod - y and limb; And the Lord will de -

liv - er you and me If we on - ly trust in him.

SINGER: *(Sees* NATHAN.*)* Tell me, my friend, how did you like my song?

NATHAN: It was OK, I guess. But I don't really go for that stuff about Daniel in the lions' den. That's for Sunday school kids.

SINGER: You've got something against Daniel?

NATHAN: No, nothing in particular. If there ever was a Daniel, and if he got in and out of that lions' den, more power to him. But he should have had my worries! They're worse than a den of lions, let me tell you.

SINGER: But what's bothering you?

NATHAN: Well, you see there's this little. . . . No, the whole thing's too personal to talk about.

SINGER: That's all right. If you've got something personal bothering you, tell it to a stranger. He won't pop up five years later and remind you of what you said.

NATHAN: Guess you're right. And I do need to talk to somebody—although I don't suppose it'll do any good.

SINGER: Can't do any harm. Come over here. Sit down and tell me your troubles. (*Indicates seat beside him.* NATHAN *sits down.*)

NATHAN: Well, to begin with, you gotta understand I've got no complaints against my wife. She's the best little woman in the world.

SINGER: Oh-oh. Seems like I've heard this story before. The people who get into trouble always seem to have the best little wives in the world. Or else they're married to the worst old hags that ever lived.

NATHAN: I guess you're right. Anyway, my wife is good—too good for me, I suppose. We've been married 15 years—*15 happy years.* And suddenly I feel restless, unhappy—it's almost as if I've become another person.

SINGER: And you've met another woman who fascinates you.

NATHAN: How—how did you guess that?

SINGER: (*Smiles.*) Just lucky, I suppose.

NATHAN: Well, you're right. There's a woman in the office where I work. She's younger than I am and I suppose I shouldn't even pay any attention to her. But somehow she's exciting, fascinating, in a way my wife isn't any more. Gloria teases and tantalizes me and makes me feel young again. She's ... she's. ... Oh, God, I wish I'd never met her.

SINGER: Why do you say that? There's nothing wrong with being young and interesting.

NATHAN: But she's interesting to *me*. That's the trouble. Oh, I haven't done anything wrong yet. But I'm tempted, tempted all the time. I keep thinking that I want to leave my wife, that I want to divorce her and marry Gloria.

SINGER: You think that would make you happy?

NATHAN: (*Stands up and paces back and forth.*) I don't know. I don't know. It's all crazy, mixed up. Sometimes I want to leave my job and get away from this temptation, and sometimes I want to leave my wife and start life all over again with another woman. I was happy until Gloria came to work in the office. Why does God let a man be tempted like that? It's God's fault if I get into trouble. She could have gone to work someplace else.

SINGER: Sure she could have. Life could have turned out a dozen different ways. But it turned out this way for you. Blaming God won't help.

NATHAN: OK. Go ahead, preach to me. Tell me that

what I'm thinking of doing is wrong. I'll listen.
But you won't make any speeches that I haven't
already made to myself. And they haven't helped
a bit.

SINGER: Preaching's not my business, my friend. I'm
a singer, a singer for the Lord. Just listen to my
song about Daniel again. *(Starts to play and
sing.)*

NATHAN: Hey, wait a minute. I don't want to be sung
to. *(It's too late. The* SINGER *has started and he
sings "Daniel in the Lions' Den" again.)*

NATHAN: All right. You sang your song again, even
though I didn't like it the first time. But I tell
you, being in a lions' den isn't like what's bothering me. It was all over in one shot with Daniel.
Either the lions bit him or they didn't. But I'm
in hell every day, twisting and turning on the
devil's spit. Oh, God, I need help.

SINGER: Look, I think you've got the wrong picture
of Daniel. He had to face temptation just like
you're doing. And it was always there to chal-
lenge him, even when he wasn't threatened with
death in a lions' den.

NATHAN: Why are you so bent on talking about that
old codger?

SINGER: Because my name is Daniel. And somehow
I feel close to him, almost as if I were that ancient Israelite born into a new world. I think I
understand what he went through, how God put
him to the test and yet helped him out of the
pit. That's why I sing about him. And that's why

you should try to understand his troubles. He'll make you see the way out of yours.

NATHAN: All right, all right. I'll agree that Daniel had a pretty rough time. At least that's what the Bible says. But it doesn't say he had any Persian dancing girls bothering him. So how does his story help me?

SINGER: Patience, my friend. Sit down again. (NATHAN *sits.*) First let me refresh your memory about Daniel. My great namesake was a man with a good reputation, so good that the king of Persia honored him more than all other government officials. And that made them jealous.

NATHAN: I can understand that. There's more jealousy in government or in business offices than in half the marriages in this country.

SINGER: You're probably right. But Daniel's enemies were driven by their jealousy to set a trap for him. They got the king to agree that for 30 days no one was to pray to any god or man except the king.

NATHAN: That was a dumb law if I ever heard one!

SINGER: Yes, but it flattered the king's vanity. Somehow, he forgot that Daniel prayed three times a day to his own God. And the penalty for doing that was to be thrown into a den of hungry lions.

NATHAN: Nice people they had in those days. But Daniel had a simple choice—yes or no. Either he had to obey the king or keep on with his prayers. That was an easy decision.

SINGER: You make it sound too simple. Decisions are never easy. Daniel had to face temptation and wrestle with himself, just as you're doing now. *(Gets up and walks to center of stage.)* Here, let me show you what I mean. I'll be the real Daniel for a little while and let you see my tempters. *(Snaps fingers and the* FIRST TEMPTER *appears. The* SINGER *is now assuming the character of Daniel and his voice and gestures are different.)*

NATHAN: Say, how did you do that? What kind of a trick is this?

DANIEL (SINGER): Don't ask questions. For a few minutes the door of the past is open to you. Look and learn.

FIRST TEMPTER: *(Swaggers a bit.)* Well, well, Daniel. You're on the spot, aren't you? It's the lions' den for you if you say your prayers today. I've been warning you about being too religious.

DANIEL: My enemies are only using my religion to attack me. They are plotting against my life.

FIRST TEMPTER: Of course they are. Nobody likes a pious fool. But with all your so-called wisdom, you are an idiot to let religion get you into a scrape like this.

DANIEL: I'm not asking anything except to be allowed to worship the true God.

FIRST TEMPTER: The true god. That's good. Everybody thinks his god is the true one. But Daniel, religion ought to help you, not make you miserable. You're going to end up as a failure, man, if you don't stop being so serious about religion. Look at it this way—all men like to succeed in business or at games or with women. To do that you've got to stretch your principles a bit now and then. After all, who's hurt if you do forget to pray for 30 days or so?

DANIEL: God will be hurt.

FIRST TEMPTER: God? You can't hurt him.

DANIEL: Oh, yes you can. God has been good to me. He helped me become a leader in Babylon and then raised me to an even more important place here in Persia. I would be guilty of gross ingratitude if I turned against God now. But I have no intention of denying him, even if it costs me my life.

FIRST TEMPTER: That's all wrong, Daniel. Such a waste, if you were to die over a silly little thing like this. Why can't you do what comes naturally? Save your life. Don't let religion rob you of the good things of this world.

DANIEL: It's never wrong to do right. Get out of my life, tempter. You've been at me every step of the way, always urging me to take the easy way and be like the Babylonians and the Persians. Leave me. Leave me. I serve my God in good weather and in bad. I'm not frightened by lions. I'm only fearful that I might fail God. Get away from me.

FIRST TEMPTER: *(Going off stage.)* You'll be sorry—sorry.

NATHAN: Say, you really told that tempter off. I mean, Daniel did. Oh, I'm all mixed up. But I'm beginning to see a little light. God's been good to me too. I shouldn't repay his goodness by messing up my life just because I'm tempted with this woman. But I'm afraid, afraid. Oh, deliver me from evil, God.

SINGER: There were other tempters, too, who assailed Daniel. Watch and listen. (*Assumes* DANIEL *character and snaps fingers.*)

SECOND TEMPTER: (*Appears from stage left.*) Hah, Daniel, let me touch you. (TEMPTER *does so.*) Let me feel you. Your flesh is firm and warm. (*Feels pulse.*) I can even feel the blood pulsing through your veins. It's good to be alive, isn't it Daniel?

DANIEL: I've never thought otherwise.

SECOND TEMPTER: No. I'm sure you haven't. But this time tomorrow the sun will shine again in this city. The hot breeze will strike people on their cheeks. It will be followed later by the cooling wind. People will sip cooling glasses of wine and taste the melons from the countryside. But you'll not see or feel or taste anything, Daniel. (*Harshly.*) Because your blood will be splattered all over the floor of the lions' den. You'll be dead, Daniel —dead, dead, dead! Have you thought of that?

DANIEL: I've thought of little else the past few days.

SECOND TEMPTER: Oh, it's good to be alive, Daniel. To breathe the air of the earth, to feel the heat of the sun, to see the shadows of evening creep across the landscape and then to see the pale light of the moon. Life is good, Daniel! A man ought to enjoy the earth while he can.

DANIEL: I've never hated life. A man should enjoy the days God gives him.

SECOND TEMPTER: Yes, because you're a long time dead. Don't be a fool, man! Forget about your prayers for a few days. What difference will it make to God in his bright heaven if he doesn't hear your voice for a little while? He's not keeping score. He may not even notice if you don't pray at all.

DANIEL: I will notice it. If I do what is wrong, I will have to live with that for the rest of my life. It will scar me and destroy me.

SECOND TEMPTER: Ah, how well you talk. Your mind is bent on playing the hero. You want to do the right thing and be noble and religious. But your body is treacherous, isn't it? It wants to live. If you listen to your body, if you consult your flesh, you'll have a better answer to what you should do.

DANIEL: A human being isn't the plaything of his mind or his emotions. I serve the God who has loved me and blessed me. You cannot destroy me by appealing to the coward that lies within everyone. I intend to do what is right. Go away, tempter. You will not beat me down, because my God delivers me from evil. Go, go, you with your seductive words and your poisonous tongue. Go! (SECOND TEMPTER *leaves.*)

NATHAN: Wow! That's telling them off.

SINGER: *(Back in character.)* Do you see why I said Daniel might be of help to you?

NATHAN: Yes. I understand that part about man's treacherous flesh. Every time I get my mind made up to leave Gloria alone, my body cuts away my fine resolutions. And when my body seems to be winning, my conscience spoils it all by reminding me I will have to live with what I do. Why, why am I put to such a test?

SINGER: Who knows why God lets us be tested? He never takes us into his confidence.

NATHAN: Maybe there isn't any God. Maybe life is simply a battle between body and mind, between the good and evil in human beings.

SINGER: Daniel faced that temptation too. Let me show you. (*Snaps fingers and assumes the role of* DANIEL.)

THIRD TEMPTER: *(Appears from stage left.)* Well, Daniel, you've decided to be stubborn, haven't you?

DANIEL: I've decided to do what is right.

THIRD TEMPTER: *(Bows.)* I salute you. You're a marvelous gambler.

DANIEL: I don't gamble. I don't have time for foolish games.

THIRD TEMPTER: Oh, yes, you're a gambler all right. One of the boldest I've ever known! You're gambling your whole life on a theory.

DANIEL: What do you mean by that?

THIRD TEMPTER: You're risking everything by praying to a God who may not even exist.

DANIEL: I know God exists. He is the one who has watched over me all my life. He is the one who raised me from a poor captive in Babylon to become the king's chief minister in Persia. You cannot shake my faith.

THIRD TEMPTER: Can't I? How noble! But perhaps you can explain some things to me then. If there is a God who cares for his people on earth, how can there be evil in this world? Why doesn't God get rid of it, if he has the power? If there is a God, how is it that you who worship him are exiled from your home while the impious in Persia lie safe in their beds? How is it that the crooked men who are plotting against you seem about to win out while you are going to be thrown into a den of lions? How is it that thieves and robbers go free while good men and women often suffer in prison or live lives of poverty and hunger? Explain that, if you can.

DANIEL: I do not pretend to know God's mind or understand his ways. I only know I believe in him and serve him.

THIRD TEMPTER: And if you're wrong?

DANIEL: Then I'm wrong. But I'll stake my life on

God. And if that's gambling, then I am a gambler.

THIRD TEMPTER: And if you lose your gamble, you'll have thrown away your life for nothing except an idle theory. Isn't it better, Daniel, to live and enjoy what you have here? If there is a God, he'll hardly begrudge you a few pleasures. And if he doesn't exist, you will at least have enjoyed the good things of the world.

DANIEL: You strike hard at me, tempter.

THIRD TEMPTER: Look, gambler, the odds are all on my side now.

DANIEL: A lot of people will agree with you. But you forget one thing.

THIRD TEMPTER: What?

DANIEL: If you are wrong, then I have destroyed myself. I would rather face a den of lions than stand before God after I have denied him.

THIRD TEMPTER: So you would destroy yourself because of the remote chance that God lives and judges?

DANIEL: No, I will live my life as a witness to God's goodness. I will be safer in his care than I am when I live in the king's palace. For though God may let a man be tested, he delivers his servants from evil. Go away, tempter! It's time for me to pray and for my enemies to watch me and accuse me. I don't know what tomorrow will bring, but today I will do what is right despite what anyone says. Go, leave me alone.

THIRD TEMPTER: Daniel, you'll be sorry.

FIRST and SECOND TEMPTER: *(Offstage.)* Daniel, you'll be sorry.

DANIEL: *(Kneels.)* O God of Abraham, Isaac, and Jacob *(Fades out.)*

NATHAN: *(Shakes him.)* What kind of trickery are you using on me, Singer? *(SINGER arises.)* Your tempters have not been talking to Daniel, but to me. They have plucked my brain and stolen every argument that I was using to excuse my sinful desires. How could you fool me like this, pretending to be Daniel when all the while I was the one you were talking to?

SINGER: Evil doesn't change much, my friend. *(Walks back to stage left.)* But God doesn't change either. He is still ready to help when we are tempted.

NATHAN: Well, I should thank you, anyway. I think I have learned my lesson. I'll be strong now. The temptation is all past.

SINGER: Be careful, man. Evil doesn't yield that quickly.

*(TEMPTERS rush back on stage and surround NATHAN. They poke at him and yell.)*

FIRST TEMPTER: Ha, Nathan! So you think you've learned your lesson, do you. I'll show you. Daniel escaped us. And he's dead now. But as long as you live you are our target. We'll tempt you and tease you and worry you day and night.

SECOND TEMPTER: I'll make your flesh strong and your mind weak. I'll be with you all the time, giving you lustful thoughts, conjuring up evil pictures, making you cry after what you do not have.

THIRD TEMPTER. Doubts, fears, troubles, boredom— these are my weapons against you. And you are only a weak human being, while I have caught thousands like you before.

NATHAN: Help me, help me, singer! Drive them away!

SINGER: I'm not the one who can help. But I'll sing my song again and maybe you'll learn where help is to be found.

*(While* SINGER *is singing the song,* TEMPTERS *dance around* NATHAN, *seeking to strike him and grab him. He manages to ward them off.)*

NATHAN: Oh God, don't lead me into any more temptation. Deliver me from the evil that is attacking me. I ask it in the name of Jesus, who died for me. (TEMPTERS *leave.)* Why, why, they're gone! All of them.

SINGER: They will be back, my friend.

NATHAN: I know they will. I'm beginning to realize that temptation is always here for me—and for everyone else. Evil lurks at every turn. And God lets it happen. I don't understand that. But there is always a way of escape. God will help me, just as he helped Daniel who faced a den of lions, just as he helped Jesus through the dark hours of Gethsemane, just as he has helped millions who have called on him for help. (SINGER *leaves during this speech.*) Thank you, Singer, showing me the way and teaching me to trust in God when I'm tempted. *(Looks around.)* Why—why—where is he? *(To audience.)* He's gone. Vanished. Was he some kind of messenger God sent to me? Was he real, or just a figment of my mind? I'm all confused. But I'm clear about one thing. God, who loves me through Jesus Christ, can and will deliver me from evil. Praise be to him, now and forever.

# *Into Deeper Waters*

"And lead us not into temptation,
But deliver us from evil."

At the opening of the Book of Job, God and Satan are pictured together, like two old cronies, conspiring to subject Job to a series of trials and temptations. It is a puzzlesome, disturbing opening for a tremendous book. Even if we decide to interpret this part as drama and not actual history, the scene still troubles us.

The words of the Lord's Prayer about temptation only add to our bewilderment. "Lead us not into temptation." Does God do such a thing? Does he operate in a conspiracy with Satan? In his Small Catechism, Martin Luther insists that God tempts no one to sin. Luther can rely on the epistle of James for this truth (although the reformer didn't have a high regard for the epistle). James writes: "Let no one say when he is tempted, 'I am tempted by God'; for God . . . tempts no one" (1:13). And yet the words of the Lord's Prayer stand.

Part of the trouble arises from confusion of two expressions — *trials* and *temptations*. Often both words are used to describe the same experience, but they are very different. Every human being must face trials in this life. All of us have our faith put to the test. We are upset by the death of a loved one. Sickness may rob us of our strength. A business failure may plunge us into despair. The list of trials is endless. But these trials also become temptations. Job's troubles made him want to die. A business failure may make us lose our sense of purpose in life. Every trial may serve to drive us away from God.

Of course the opposite may also be true. We may emerge from a temptation stronger and more appreciative of our faith. Peter compares our suffering to the fire used to refine gold and points out that the gold is better for having been through the fiery refinement process. Nevertheless as human beings we cannot be expected to want to suffer in this world. We are not expected to ask God to make us sick or to take away someone dear to us so we can be stronger Christians. So the prayer petition is a proper one and shows how completely Jesus understood human nature. We ask God not to put us to the test. We would rather not be tempted.

But we know this prayer isn't going to be answered completely. In the words of an old hymn

> Must Jesus bear the cross alone,
> And all the world go free?
> No, there's a cross for ev'ry one,
> And there's a cross for me.

None of us get off scot-free in this life. We all have
to face the fire sometime. We have to walk the
rocky path, we have to live through a soul-shatter-
ing experience. And so we add the rest of the
prayer: "But deliver us from evil."

What we are saying then is, "God, don't let me
get into trouble. But since I'm going to anyway,
please get me out of trouble when I get into it." It
is important that these two petitions go together.
For only if we believe God will deliver us do we
have the courage to face life with its temptations
and difficulties.

Actually these two statements tell the story of
every life. All of us want a life free of trouble. We
would like to be free of all difficulties. But life is
not like that. So we must ask for the next best. We
ask God to rescue us from the pitfalls of life. And the
word of God assures us that this part of the prayer
will always be answered. The God who delivered
Israel from a thousand troubles has promised that
we will be safe in his hands.

That tremendous passage in the eighth chapter
of Romans is the best commentary on this part of
the Lord's prayer. Paul writes:

> Who shall separate us from the love of Christ?
> Shall tribulation, or distress, or persecution, or
> famine, or nakedness, or peril or sword? . . .
> No, in all these things we are more than con-
> querors through him who loved us. For I am
> sure that neither death, nor life, nor angels, nor
> principalities, nor things present, nor things to
> come, nor powers, nor height, nor depth, nor
> anything else in all creation, will be able to sep-

arate us from the love of God in Christ Jesus our Lord (vv. 35-39).

Those words should eliminate any fear that God will not heed our prayer when we ask, "But deliver us from evil."

During war submarines are sometimes attacked by depth charges. Undoubtedly the submarine commander would prefer not to be attacked, but when attack occurs, he knows what to do. He takes his vessel deeper into the ocean where it will be safe from such charges.

We are in a similar situation. We would prefer not to have to face temptation. But when it comes, we know the answer. We must plunge deeper into God's care and concern, for true safety is found there. He both can and will deliver us from evil.

*For thine
is the kingdom,
and the power,
and the glory, for ever.*

**Matthew 6:13b (King James)**

DRAMA | *The Glory of God*

MEDITATION | *The Easter Doxology*

# The Glory of God

## CHARACTERS

LAZARUS: brother of Mary and Martha; young, sympathetic

MARY: rather dreamy-eyed, soft-spoken

MARTHA: moody, rather belligerent; a strong character

JARUS: about Lazarus' age; a bit cynical

MARY MAGDALENE: fairly young, eager

## SETTING

The scene is a house in Bethany with chairs or benches for at least four characters. A low table can be used but isn't essential.

## COSTUMES

Palestinian costumes or modern dress.

(As the play opens, MARY and MARTHA are sitting motionless as though in prayer. LAZARUS enters.)

LAZARUS: Martha—Mary! Are you two still sitting here in the house? Come out and walk in the garden with me. The whole place is flooded with sunlight and everything seems to be bursting with life.

MARY: Jesus isn't alive. And if he is dead, there isn't any life in the garden. The whole world died for me on Friday. I just want to sit here and mourn for the world.

LAZARUS: *(A bit disgusted.)* I might have known you would say something strange like that, Mary. But Martha, you at least are sensible. You don't live in your own private world. Come out of this dark house and walk for a little while in the garden. It'll do you good. The flowers you planted this year are blooming their hearts out. If flowers have hearts.

MARTHA: The last time I saw Jesus was in that garden. I will never walk there any more.

LAZARUS: All right. I tried. I won't coax either one of you. But sisters, you haven't slept or eaten for two days. You can't go on like this!

MARTHA: Lazarus, we mourned four days for you and we would have wept longer than that if Jesus hadn't brought you back to us. Do you think we'll shed fewer tears for him?

LAZARUS: *(A bit peeved.)* Sometimes I think you would have preferred that I, your own brother, had stayed dead and Jesus had lived.

MARY: Of course we would rather have it that way,

Lazarus. As long as Jesus lived, we believed you were safe, alive or dead. But with Jesus gone, who knows what to believe?

MARTHA: Jesus told me in my own garden that he was the resurrection and the life. And I was so sure he was right when he gave you back to us. But now—what am I to believe? No resurrection, no life for me anymore.

MARY: I would think you would sit and mourn too, Lazarus. After all, you owe your life to him.

LAZARUS: *(Angry.)* Don't you think I know that! Just the thought of Jesus being dead cuts sharper than the pain did before I died. I'm only trying to cheer you up a little. It can't be right to sit here and mourn like this. Jesus wouldn't have wanted you to. He was always so full of the joy of living. And God wouldn't want you to grieve like this either.

MARTHA: God! How can we believe in God after this? I saw God in Jesus' face. I heard God speaking in Jesus' words. Now God means nothing to me—nothing!

MARY: Martha, Martha, don't say that. We've got to hold fast to something.

MARTHA: What?

MARY: I don't know yet. But at least we have memories left. For a little while someone good and loving came into our lives. For a few years we caught a glimpse of something better than this dead, broken world. We had sunlight and music and dancing in our hearts. That's all gone now, but let's remember Jesus as he was.

LAZARUS: *(Bitterly.)* Yes, as he was. What a terrible thing to have to speak of a person as "was." That's the way you talked about me for those four days I was gone, I suppose. I had become a "was." I wonder what death has meant for Jesus. I wonder if he feels the cold and the darkness the way I did, the sense of nothingness, the shadows and shapes in the tomb?

MARTHA: Don't, Lazarus! I can't bear to think of Jesus in a grave. Those eyes that looked at me with God's love in every glance—closed forever. That voice that soothed me and healed me, even when I mourned—stilled forever. I can't bear it. I won't stand for it. *(She is standing and has become hysterical.)* I know what I'll do. I'll go to Jerusalem myself and scratch out the eyes of those false men who condemned Jesus to death. I will! I will! *(She collapses in tears as the other two rush to her.)*

MARY: *(Helps her back to her seat.)* Careful, Martha. Easy, easy.

LAZARUS: Can I get you some water?

MARTHA: No, I'm all right now. I just had to let it all loose for a minute. But I feel so weak, so beaten.

LAZARUS: *(Paces, agitatedly.)* We all feel useless. I couldn't even go to Jerusalem to see him die because they were threatening my life too. Jesus could bring me out of the grave with a prayer and a command, but I was useless when his time came. Useless. Useless.

MARY: *(Softly.)* What could anyone do? His enemies had the power to kill him. The kingdom of darkness was stronger than the kingdom he talked about. How quickly it all happened. When Jesus raised you from the dead, Lazarus, I felt he could do anything he wanted to. That's why I anointed his feet with perfume. He was the king and I was one of his subjects, paying tribute to him.

MARTHA: He took it as a preparation for his burial.

MARY: I know. A cold shiver ran through my body when I heard him say that. But I didn't think he really meant it.

LAZARUS: I wonder where the others are—Peter and James and John and the rest?

MARTHA: *(Scornfully.)* Gone back to Galilee to go fishing, I suppose. A lot of good they were when he needed them.

MARY: Now, now, Martha. It's not for us to judge. A legion of soldiers can make us all cowards.

MARTHA: Oh, I'm not blaming the disciples. I'm blaming God! Where was he when it all happened?

LAZARUS: Martha, Martha, don't get yourself excited again.

MARTHA: I'm not excited. I'm icy calm. I simply

want to know where God was when Jesus hung on that cross.

LAZARUS: I heard from old Solom that there was an earthquake and a terrible storm when Jesus died. And it got very dark for awhile. God did show his anger.

MARTHA: Very touching! But God let Jesus die. Simply saying "naughty, naughty" by means of earthquakes and darkness isn't enough for me.

LAZARUS: It's very strange. I don't understand it at all.

MARTHA: I do. God deserted him, that's all!

MARY: Martha, Martha, don't say things like that. Just sit and pray. That's all I know to do.

MARTHA: *(Stands up.)* No, I've sat long enough. Jesus once scolded me for being busy in the kitchen, but maybe that's where I belong. Maybe it's time for me to get busy in my kitchen again and forget about God and death and everything else. At least work may dull the pain inside me. *(A knock on the door.)*

LAZARUS: Who can that be?

MARTHA: *(Tartly.)* The best way to find out is to open the door.

LAZARUS: You're right as usual, big sister. Maybe a visitor may help turn our minds away from grief for a little while. *(Goes to the door and is shocked at what he sees.)* Jarus!

JARUS: *(Still outside.)* Lazarus, may I come in?

LAZARUS: Why I—I suppose so. It's been a long while since we've seen you. But come in. (JARUS *enters.* MARTHA *takes hold of* LAZARUS.)

MARTHA: No, no, Lazarus! Don't let him in! Jarus has come to gloat over our sorrow. And we don't need that now. Please don't let him stay.

JARUS: *(Jokes a bit.)* Still the same Martha, aren't you, fighting like a mother cat defending her favorite kitten. Only this time the kitten is dead. Well, am I in or out?

MARY: Jesus taught us to love even our enemies. How can we refuse to talk to an old friend like Jarus? Even though he hasn't been very friendly to us lately.

MARTHA: I want to know what he wants here. Today of all days.

JARUS: Look, Martha, Mary, Lazarus — we were friends for a long while. We quarreled over *your* friend, Jesus. You thought he was a true prophet; I thought he was a false one. Now he's dead, so it doesn't make any difference anymore. I thought I would come by today and renew our friendship. But if you want me to go. . . .

MARTHA: *(Takes* JARUS *by the hand and leads him to a seat beside herself.)* I spoke too quickly, Jarus. Come and sit down. I'll prepare something for us to eat.

JARUS: You haven't changed a bit, Martha. Still the

best cook in Bethany and determined to prove it. Come, sit down and talk to me a little while. The food can wait.

MARTHA: *(Sits down.)* Strange—you sound like Jesus when you say that. He didn't want me to spend time working in the kitchen either.

LAZARUS: *(Sits down.)* You must be patient with us, Jarus. The death of Jesus has dealt us a hard blow. We all find it difficult to talk about anything else or even think about anything else today.

JARUS: I understand. And I will grant you this much. Your prophet died like a good man. He even called on God to receive his spirit when he died. It was very touching.

MARTHA: *(Aroused again.)* You saw him die! You were with that crowd that mocked him and spat on him! If you tell me you were there, I'll do some spitting myself.

JARUS: *(Laughs.)* Oh-oh, I've set her off again. Look, Martha, I had nothing to do with Jesus' death, although it was obvious that it was going to happen. You don't offend the high priest's party without having to pay for it. But I was in Jerusalem this past week and I watched the whole brutal business. Those hypocritical, evil priests!

MARY: For goodness sake, Jarus, whose side are you on? You always sneered when we talked about Jesus. That's why Martha forbade you to come here. Now you seem to be taking Jesus' part. And a lot of good that does, now that he's dead.

JARUS: I don't take anybody's part, Mary. I just like to sit and watch what goes on. And I sneer because I think everybody takes religion too seriously in this land. You three thought you had found the Messiah when you met this Galilean. Some Messiah, talking about a vague kingdom that was coming or was already here. I'll admit that he performed a few dubious miracles but those things didn't convince me. I'm sorry he had to die, but Lazarus, you helped cause his death, aided and abetted by your clever sisters here.

LAZARUS: What do you mean by that?

JARUS: Oh, you know as well as I do. Lazarus, your clever resurrection created such a stir in the city that the priests felt they had to get rid of Jesus before he took charge and began giving them orders. But I'll admit the resurrection was a master stroke. Look, it can't do any harm now. How about telling me how you managed all this?

MARTHA: *(Menacingly.)* Are you saying what I think you're saying?

JARUS: *(Unaware of the change in the atmosphere.)* I don't know, Martha. I can't read your mind. But you three certainly did manage to pull off a perfect stunt designed to impress everyone with Jesus' power. I congratulate you for your cleverness. It was done with such rare dramatic taste—the message to Jesus, his delay in coming to you, the fake death, Martha's reluctance to order her brother's tomb reopened, and finally the bound figure appearing and frightening practically everyone out of their wits. Oh, it was done marvelously! I wish I had been here and watched you carrying out the whole plan.

MARTHA: *(Seizes him.)* Jarus, get out! You can't pretend to be a friend of ours and then sit here calmly and accuse us of trickery.

JARUS: But I'm complimenting you! You did a marvelous job. I heard the whole story from a friend of mine, and he was completely taken in. Everything was done with perfect timing. Did Jesus plan all this or were you the brains behind it, Mary? I suspect your dreamy mind and your clever hand controlled the whole show.

MARTHA: I say, get out!

MARY: *(Taking charge.)* Be quiet, Martha. Don't you realize that a man who believes in nothing will call even the truth a lie? Jarus, there was no trickery. You understand? No trickery! Lazarus was dead for four days and now he's alive. God gave him back to us through Jesus.

JARUS: You can't be serious. Lazarus, tell me the truth.

LAZARUS: You're hearing the truth. I was dead. Dead. And now I'm alive.

MARTHA: My tears weren't fake, Jarus. If you had been here, even you would have known that my grief was real.

JARUS: But this is incredible. It can't be true!

LAZARUS: It is true. Jesus raised me from the dead. It's as simple as that.

JARUS: Ah, the weak spot in your armor. Look, friends, there's no use in continuing this fooling. Jesus himself is dead. I saw the spear thrust in his side. The soldiers didn't break his legs because they knew he was already dead, and you don't fool those soldiers. How could Jesus raise you from the dead and then not lift a hand to save himself from the cross? What good can you hope to accomplish by clinging to this fantasy of a messiah who can raise the dead?

MARTHA: If you had any sense, Jarus, you'd see that it isn't a fantasy. We're telling you the truth. But you've put your finger on the thing that's driving us mad. How could Jesus raise up Lazarus and then end up a dead man himself? There have been times in the past few days when I might have listened to your crazy idea that Jesus was a false prophet. But false prophets don't raise the dead. And yet, why is Jesus in the grave now? The only thing that makes sense to me is that God himself is dead.

MARY: Martha, don't say such things! Jarus, can't you see that our whole life has collapsed? We had such faith in Jesus. We believed he would set up God's kingdom here on this earth.

JARUS: I'm beginning to think you are serious.

LAZARUS: We're not lying to you, Jarus. I felt the power of Jesus flow into my dead body and make me alive again. But it wasn't just that.

Everything that Jesus said and did revealed
God to us. I know you didn't want to listen to
him, but if you had, you would have known
that he was a true prophet, in fact the Messiah
himself. But how could the Messiah die? That's
what's tearing us apart. There doesn't seem to
be any purpose to life anymore. I've been trying to get Mary and Martha at least to walk
outside and look at God's world, but they won't
even stir.

MARY: There's a time to grieve, and this is the time.
Only I don't see how we can ever stop grieving!

JARUS: I'm afraid to say what I've been thinking.

MARTHA: Go on, say it. Say "I told you so." You
can't make us feel any worse.

JARUS: It's not that. But I heard something in the
city that almost begins to make sense, and yet—

MARY: Do you have any news, Jarus? Speak, man, if
you know anything that might make us feel better. Are Jesus' followers rallying? Is there talk
of an uprising?

JARUS: Nothing like that.

LAZARUS: It would be too late, anyway.

MARTHA: Jarus, you know something. Tell us! *(They
have him surrounded.)*

JARUS: No, I don't want to raise any false hopes.

MARTHA: *(Seizes him and almost chokes him.)* Tell
us, man!

JARUS: All right. I did hear something in Jerusalem just before I left there this morning. But I didn't pay any attention to what people said because I was convinced Jesus was a fraud and that you people arranged the whole business of raising Lazarus from the dead. But if there was no trick—

LAZARUS: There was no trick.

MARTHA: Get on with it, Jarus!

JARUS: All right. There's a rumor in the city that Jesus' tomb is empty. They say his body is gone. There was a guard in front of the stone last night, but the men ran away from their post, babbling about an angel appearing and frightening them.

MARTHA: Someone has stolen the body. Or—

MARY: He is alive. Suddenly I feel it in my heart. And my heart has never been wrong about Jesus.

LAZARUS: Let's not jump to conclusions. Still, if he raised me from the dead—

MARTHA: Lazarus, get ready at once. You must go to Jerusalem and find out about all this.

MARY: You forget—some of the priests wanted to kill Lazarus too. His life may still be in danger.

MARTHA: Lazarus must run the risk.

JARUS: I'll go back, if it would be any help to you.

MARY: No, only Jesus' disciples will know the truth. And they wouldn't talk to you.

LAZARUS: How could Peter or James forget to tell us if anything has happened? We've always been so close to all of them.

JARUS: I only said it was a rumor. You know how people talk. There may be nothing to it.

MARY: There is something to it—I'm sure of that. I'll go and find out.

MARTHA: What! You're so dreamy you can't even boil an egg! You're the last one in the family to go on an errand like this.

MARY: Don't try to keep me back. If Jesus is alive, I can face lions! *(Heads for the door. At the same time there is knocking at the door.)*

MARTHA: Now who can that be? Lazarus, open the door.

LAZARUS: What a time for an interruption! *(Opens door.)* Why, Mary Magdalene, what are you doing here?

MAGDALENE: *(Out of breath.)* Let me sit down for a moment. *(They lead her to a seat.)* Great news! Great news! I've got to get my breath first. But I can't wait to tell it. I ran almost all the way from Jerusalem. *(Gasping.)*

MARTHA: Here, let me get you a cup of water.

MAGDALENE: No, no. I'll be all right. Friends— *(Catches sight of JARUS.)* Oh, who is that?

LAZARUS: It's Jarus, an old acquaintance. You can speak in front of him—I think.

JARUS: You can trust me. And I hope you have some real good news. This family has been saddened by the death of their friend, Jesus.

MAGDALENE: That's my news. Jesus isn't dead any more! He's alive! *(Stands up.)*

ALL: What!

MARY: *(Hugs her.)* Are you sure, Magdalene?

MAGDALENE: I've seen him! I've talked to him! I thought he was the gardener, but it was Jesus.

JARUS: You're all excited. You don't know what you're saying.

MAGDALENE: Oh yes I do! Jesus has come back from the grave. God has raised him up. Oh Mary, Martha, Lazarus—we were all such fools to doubt Jesus, to forget his promises, to grieve for him. He's alive, he's alive!

MARTHA: O God, forgive me for being such a fool. I should have known Jesus was safe in your hands. God, forgive me!

LAZARUS: Hah, now he will set up his kingdom! He will show the whole world that he is the Messiah.

MARY: Perhaps not just the way we think, Lazarus. We're going to have to stop trying to say what he should do. But glory to God for this good news.

JARUS: Wait a minute. Don't get carried away like this.

MAGDALENE: Why not, my friend?

JARUS: Because a Messiah has to do more than perform miracles, even as great a miracle as rising from the dead.

MAGDALENE: He has already shown what kind of a Lord he is. He saved me from seven devils and made me a God-loving woman. That took more power than all his healing of people's bodies. And I have seen his face since God has raised him up and he shines like the sun at midday. And I have heard his voice, the same kind loving voice he had before. He did not reproach me for my doubts or blame me for my sins. I'll give my life for such a Messiah.

MARTHA: Now I can invite Jesus down to our home again. I'll prepare him a feast like he's never had before!

MAGDALENE: *(Slowly.)* I don't think so, Martha. I think he'll give all the feasts from now on.

LAZARUS: We must get down on our knees and thank God for this. This is a better day than the one when Jesus brought me back to life. Now it means life for all of us!

MARTHA: Yes. Now I know he is the resurrection and the life.

JARUS: Do you think—do you think I could join in that prayer with you! Suddenly my cold heart seems strangely warmed. Would Jesus accept my prayers?

MARY: More than your prayers, Jarus, Jesus would accept you. And we will all accept you as a brother if you learn to love our Jesus.

JARUS: I think I'm beginning to love him already. Forgive me, Lord, for being so slow to accept you.

LAZARUS: Glory be to God for this day!

# The Easter Doxology

"For thine is the kingdom, and the power, and the glory, for ever. Amen" (King James).

This beautiful doxology was apparently not part of the Lord's Prayer when Jesus gave it to his disciples. It was added by the early church when they began to use the prayer as a part of the worship service. Even though the words may not have been spoken by Jesus, we treasure them today. They seem to sum up our faith in God as the Father of our Lord Jesus Christ. This is the Easter doxology, the confession of the church to a Savior who not only taught his disciples how to pray but who also passed through death and resurrection to bring life to all of us.

Let's look at each of the three key words to this conclusion and see how each one reflects all that we believe and proclaim at Easter. We will find that although each word has meaning in itself, it is greatly enhanced when we think of it in the light of that first Easter. The key to this doxology is an empty tomb and a risen Savior.

We begin with *kingdom.* We have heard that word before in the Lord's Prayer. "Thy kingdom come," we pray, and thus bear testimony to a longing for a world where God rules and women and men obey. But we are aware that there is the shadow of a different world, a world where the ruler is not God and the kingdom is totally evil. And throughout human history these two kingdoms have been at war.

Jesus Christ came preaching about God's kingdom, but from the very beginning of his life the powers of darkness opposed him. He was a refugee from his homeland before he was two years old. All during his ministry there were those who opposed his kingdom and tried to discredit him. And at last that dark kingdom seemed victorious. On Good Friday Jesus was dead and his dream of a kingdom was shattered. The enemies of God no doubt exulted in their triumph.

What a difference Easter made. On that day God showed that evil did not have the last word. The kingdom of Satan was not able to mock God. In the words of an old hymn:

> Up from the grave He arose,
> With a mighty triumph o'er His foes;
> He arose a victor from the dark domain,
> And He lives forever with His saints to reign.
> He arose! He arose! Hallelujah! Christ arose!

And that's why we can say, "Thine is the kingdom." For God showed his strength on Easter. He made it possible for us to live in his kingdom forever.

"And thine is the *power.*" No one should ever doubt God's power, for if he has no power he is not

God. From the beginning God was the creator, bringing worlds into being by his word. And in human history God has demonstrated his power by setting up rulers and pulling down nations.

But human beings have always known a power that seemed stronger than God, the power of death. From Adam to Christ, death seemed invincible. Nothing in the universe seemed proof against death. Every person, every plant and animal seemed under the thumb of death. As Shakespeare put it:

> Golden lads and girls all must
> As chimney-sweepers, come to dust.

Death seemed to have the real power in the world. It is called in the Bible the last enemy of mankind.

And then came Easter. God snapped death's power that day. The strong Man of God came out of the tomb. What evidence that God rules over all things! No wonder Paul exults: "O death, where is thy sting? O grave, where is thy victory?" (1 Cor. 15:55, KJV). No wonder the creatures of heaven worship God and say, "Amen! Blessing and glory and wisdom and thanksgiving and honor and power and might be to our God for ever and ever! Amen" (Rev. 7:12). Easter is the greatest witness to God's power in all of Scripture.

"And the *glory*." A strange word, *glory*. We all know what it means but it is hard to define. The word seems to speak of dazzling light, flags waving, and bands playing. And of course the universe in which we live has much that testifies to God's glory. A spectacular sunset, a starry night, a shimmering rainbow, all can speak of the splendor of the Creator.

But Easter doesn't seem to possess much glory. True, there was an earthquake and an angel whose countenance was like lightning. But after that, things settled down to routine. The real glory of God does not lie in spectacular physical effects but in changed lives, in the father-child relationship between God and human beings. As Mr. Zuss says in Archibald MacLeish' play, *J.B.,* "It's God the Father I play— not God the boiling point of water."

You and I are the glory of God. People whose lives have been transformed by Christ are the glory of God. For God is love and his love is best shown in the lives of human beings.

And so the Lord's Prayer ends with a great doxology of praise that is the message of Easter. Each time that we pray the Lord's Prayer, we should be reminded of the one who first prayed it, the one who made it possible for us to call God "Our Father."

"For thine is the kingdom, and the power, and the glory, for ever. Amen."